Identifying American Furniture

Identifying American Furniture

A Pictorial Guide to
Styles and Terms,
Colonial to Contemporary

Milo M. Naeve

The American Association for State and Local History

Nashville, Tennessee

Second Printing 1982

Publication of this book was made possible in part by funds from the
sale of the Bicentennial State Histories, which were supported by
the National Endowment for the Humanities.

Library of Congress Cataloguing-in-Publication Data

Naeve, Milo M.
  Identifying American furniture.

  Bibliography: p.
  Includes index.
    1. Furniture—United States.   2. Decoration and ornament—
United States—Themes, motives.   I. American Association for
State and Local History.   II. Title.
NK2405.N28   749.213   81-3524
ISBN 0-910050-52-X   AACR2

Contents

Preface   7
Styles

    Medieval Style, 1607–1700   **13**
    Renaissance Style, 1607–1700   **15**
    Restoration Style, 1660–1700   **17**
    William and Mary Style, 1690–1730   **19**
    Queen Anne Style, 1725–1760   **21**
    Chippendale Style, 1760–1790   **23**
    Federal Style, 1790–1815   **25**
    Classical Styles, 1805–1830   **27**
    French Restauration Style, 1830–1850   **29**
    Gothic Revival Style, 1840–1860   **31**
    Elizabethan Style, 1850–1915   **33**
    Rococo Revival Style, 1845–1870   **35**
    Naturalistic Style, 1850–1865   **37**
    Louis XVI Style, 1850–1914   **39**
    Renaissance Revival Style, 1850–1880   **41**
    Neo-Greek Style, 1855–1885   **43**
    Egyptian Revival Style, 1865–1890   **45**
    Eastlake Style, 1870–1890   **47**
    Art Furniture Styles, 1880–1914   **49**
    Arts and Crafts Styles, 1895–1915   **51**
    Art Nouveau Style, 1896–1914   **53**
    Art Deco Styles, 1925–1945   **55**
    International Style, 1940–Present   **57**

    Craftsman and Contemporary Styles, 1945–Present   **59**
    Dutch Style, 1624–1860   **61**
    German Style, 1750–1870   **63**
    Spanish Style, 1600–1900   **65**
    Vernacular Styles, 1670–1790   **67**
    Vernacular Styles, 1791–1914   **69**
    Shaker Style, 1800–1914   **71**
    Windsor Style, 1750–Present   **73**
    Garden Furniture Styles, 1800–1914   **75**

Further Reading
    Periodicals   **77**
    Books and Articles   **77**
        Background Sources: Architecture and Design   **77**
        General Sources: American Furniture   **77**
        Regional Sources: Mid-Atlantic   **79**
        Regional Sources: Midwest   **80**
        Regional Sources: New England   **80**
        Regional Sources: South   **81**
        Regional Sources: Southwest   **82**
        Regional Sources: West   **82**
Index   **83**

Preface

Styles in this handbook have swept nearly four centuries of designers, craftsmen, or patrons on the invisible winds of taste. They sometimes are an abrupt gale over a generation and sometimes a steady breeze over many.

I tried several times in several ways putting these constantly shifting and often elusive trends into a rational order in accordance with the first proposal for the project, made by Gary Gore, Director of Publications for the American Association for State and Local History. The Association wanted a succinct guide for identifying the style of a specific example, yet a broad survey for styles throughout our history. I declined.

The reasons are not mysterious. For one, the two objectives seemed contradictory. For another, I was greatly concerned at the time with very specific research on American paintings, and Gary's proposed project seemed to confirm a conclusion evident wherever curiosity erratically has led me, whether to the efforts of painters, sculptors, architects, silversmiths, potters, glassblowers, or cabinetmakers: our knowledge of the past is incomplete. It is formed by the accident of survival for documentary evidence and for works of art coupled with the even more whimsical chance encounter with either source. A responsible survey in a distilled form seemed unlikely.

The idea haunted me, however, because I often come across the need for the kind of publication that the AASLH proposed. Finally, we agreed on the venture. Like all fine publishers, mine is also a gambler. Gary has proven my greatest ally, in giving complete freedom for translating his broad proposal into my specific approach. Our only foundation was that style, the appearance of furniture, is the most useful way of bringing clarity to a complex subject.

For that reason, the illustrations are the main elements of my survey. They are on the book's left-hand pages, for convenient reference, either for finding a style of interest or in comparing it with others for similarities or differences.

They are complemented in several ways. Superimposed numbers on each illustration identify stylistic elements that are listed on the right-hand page, with a brief essay about the style. The over-all number given to each picture (Fig. 1, Fig. 2, etc.) is a key to specific information in the illustration notes on the lower part of the right-hand page.

A selection of periodicals, books, and articles in the section titled "Further Reading" completes the book. It offers a resource for specific inquiries from several points of view.

The user of this guide will find that looking through the illustrations is often his best kind of index, but the usual sort is included, listing the number of the illustration where significant motifs, designers, craftsmen, manufacturers, materials, terms, and constructions may be found.

Styles, then, are defined in this survey by the illustrations. Each example is a fully developed expression, and, within a style, the selections offer elements that can be found in endless variations and combinations on other furniture. Elaborate interpretations of a style are emphasized, because their echo always remains in simplifications.

Especially before the mid-nineteenth century, styles evolved and lingered at different times in different places. My dates refer to the general period of popularity.

An individual would be best served, I decided, if all of the furniture in the guide were publicly available. Owners are identified with the illustrations, but the listed sources are only a few of the many possibilities available to the reader in the United States and in England. I urge complementing this guide with study of actual examples.

The greatest challenge in this survey has been to attain a balance between brevity and length. Styles have emerged in many different communities and areas that could be considered individually or treated as part of a broader trend. Most of my decisions are obvious. Others are personal, about the character of trends or the identification of trends that I believe will be useful to the greatest number of readers. There are, for example, separate categories for the Rococo Revival Style and the Naturalistic Style in the mid-nineteenth century: they are related, but they differ. The many interpretations of Neo-Classical motifs and forms in the early nineteenth century, as well as furniture in the Arts and Crafts styles in the early twentieth century and the later Art Deco styles, are placed in three general categories. Variations within these styles would be treated separately, in a detailed publication; but in this survey, they are grouped as expressions of general themes. What should be done with the styles of certain European immigrants? They often are the result of "folk" or "popular" culture, but I have separated them into Dutch, German, and Spanish traditions and excluded the distinctive French and Scandinavian furniture only because examples are few in number and less likely to concern the usual reader. Eccentric combinations of several styles among rural and urban craftsmen that are independent of sophisticated styles are identified as "vernacular" styles, and examples were selected for demonstrating possibilities in the eighteenth and nineteenth centuries. I am uncomfortable with the term *vernacular*, which could refer to furniture in many degrees of simplification from sophisticated styles, but I prefer it to the inaccurate designation of *country* and the vague one of *folk*. Windsor furniture may have originated with the generation of the Revolution, but it clearly is vital in our time, and I have taken the position of including a version with Windsors instead of Contemporary Styles.

My names for styles usually are those in common use. They originated over the last century, with the revival of designs from earlier periods and with an analytical approach to the history of furniture. Inconsistencies occur in references to political periods, design sources, craftsmen, religious or national groups, and international exhibitions, but the names have the advantage of general familiarity.

American furniture rarely can be mistaken for furniture made abroad, but Americans from the seventeenth century to the present have continued the international tradition of style launched by Greeks borrowing from Egyptians and Romans from Greeks. Among many influences, English taste prevailed through the seventeenth and eighteenth centuries, English and French in the nineteenth, and French and German in the twentieth. European books and magazines directly pertinent to the evolution of American styles are mentioned in the commentaries. Their significance is documented, but equally pertinent and rarely known specifically are the influences of immigrant craftsmen, imported furniture, and patrons traveling abroad.

Technology is considered in this guide only when essential to the visual features of style. At times, technology served craftsmen with better ways of manipulating materials or achieving decorative effects. At other times, it gave craftsmen such new materials as plastics. The influence of technology, however, should not be overestimated. An innovation, such as laminated woods, might be introduced in the mid-nineteenth century and ignored until the mid-twentieth.

The advantage of a summary in a handbook of this nature bears the counterweight disadvantage of omission. Illustrations and text within these covers survey only major movements in domestic furniture. Many forms before the nineteenth century, especially bedsteads, have not survived for documenting styles completely. Innovative styles in the twentieth century are stressed over commercial adaptations and reproductions of historic styles, which are a fascinating dimension in cultural history but derivative in form and decoration.

A survey with a different accent could be published within a decade, if designers of contemporary furniture and researchers into the past continue their current vitality. But I believe my broad scheme is true now and will remain so for all who respond to the fascination of stylistic change through the years.

Milo M. Naeve

Curator, Department of American Arts
The Art Institute of Chicago

Styles

Medieval Style, 1607–1700

English medieval traditions continue in New England and in the South through ordinary furniture in houses as sparsely furnished as those abroad. There is greater evidence for the appearance of storage and seating furniture than for bedsteads, settles, or livery cupboards.

The popular slab-ended chest is made of five pine boards nailed together, with sides extended as feet and a sixth board used as the pinned or hinged top. Decoration includes incised, punched, or painted geometric designs in red, black, and white. The form occurs in England by the fourteenth century and continues in New England through the early nineteenth.

Storage boxes are as simply made and decorated as chests. Some include chip carving, known in England by the thirteenth century.

Armchairs and side chairs with rush or splint seats and turned spindles, legs, and arms differ in design and kinds of woods used from New England to the South. These types of chairs occur as early as the eleventh century in England, but the usual English and American seat during the seventeenth century is the stool.

New England furniture includes a medieval type of table with a removable top and stretcher on trestles. A version with a fixed top and stretcher continues to the early nineteenth century.

1. Turned spindles
2. Stretcher
3. Chamfer
4. Trestle base
5. Splint seat
6. Incised compass decoration
7. Cleat
8. Finial
9. Chip carving
10. Egg-and-dart motif (Renaissance Style)

1. Armchair, Connecticut, 1660–1700; ash, maple. The Art Institute of Chicago, Wirt D. Walker Fund, Chicago, Illinois.

2. Table, New England, 1640–1670; pine top, oak base. The Metropolitan Museum of Art, gift of Mrs. Russell Sage, 1909, New York, New York.

3. Armchair, Virginia or North Carolina, 1690–1720; maple, oak. The Museum of Early Southern Decorative Arts, Winston-Salem, North Carolina.

4. Six-board chest, Connecticut, 1650–1700; oak, pine, maple. Greenfield Village and Henry Ford Museum, Dearborn, Michigan.

5. Highchair for child, probably Dorchester, Massachusetts, 1640–1660; silver maple. The Art Institute of Chicago, gift of Elizabeth R. Vaughan, Chicago, Illinois.

6. Box, New Hampshire, 1674–1700, white pine. The Art Institute of Chicago, gift of Mr. Marshall Field, Mrs. C. Phillip Miller, and Mrs. Frank L. Sulzberger, Chicago, Illinois.

Renaissance Style, 1607–1700

Rectilinear oak forms with boldly curved elements and massive turnings are accented with relief carving against black, white, green, and red backgrounds. Survivals in the style of somber Renaissance splendor mainly are from New England.

Joiners secured parts with wooden pins or nailed bottom and backboards. Chests and boxes are common among the limited forms. Seating includes joint stools—a reference to joined construction—and chair-tables with backs lowering for table tops. Court cupboards offer a bottom shelf below a recessed cupboard; press cupboards are a variation, with compartments enclosing the lower section. Tables occasionally include leaves, either drawing outward or opening onto a moveable leg. Evidence is limited for bedsteads, but they probably were similar to the nineteenth-century vernacular form, and elaborate versions apparently included posts.

The Renaissance Style originated in rural England, from continental versions of the Italian Renaissance. Revived from Roman art are acanthus leaves and flowers, Doric columns, Roman arches, and torus, scotia, and astragal moldings. They merge with Renaissance circular and round feet, channel moldings, bands of notches and triangles, bulbous turnings, lunettes, foliage, attenuated leaves, bosses, grotesques, lozenges, and strapwork. Spindles, cut in half, glued together, turned, and broken apart form the common decoration known as "split spindles."

1. **Strapwork**
2. **Relief carving**
3. **Grotesque**
4. **Foliate scroll**
5. **Astragal or bead molding**
6. **Doric column**
7. **Split spindle**
8. **Boss**
9. **Lozenge**
10. **Stile**
11. **Rail**
12. **Lunette**
13. **Cleat**
14. **Roman arch** ·
15. **Muntin**
16. **Rosette**
17. **Leaf design**
18. **Channel molding**
19. **Apron or skirt**
20. **Ball foot variation**

7. Armchair, attributed to Thomas Dennis, Ipswich, Massachusetts, 1660–1675; oak. The Essex Institute, Salem, Massachusetts.

8. Joint stool, probably New Haven, Connecticut, 1640–1660; oak. The Wadsworth Atheneum, Wallace Nutting Collection, Hartford, Connecticut.

9. Press cupboard, Essex County, Massachusetts, 1675–1695; oak, pine. The Museum of Fine Arts, Boston, gift of Maurice Geeraerts, in memory of Mr. and Mrs. William R. Robeson, Boston, Massachusetts.

10. Chest, probably New Haven, Connecticut, 1640–1680; white oak, pine. The Yale University Art Gallery, the Mabel Brady Garvan Collection, New Haven, Connecticut.

11. Table, Massachusetts, 1670–1690; oak. The Wadsworth Atheneum, Wallace Nutting Collection, gift of J. P. Morgan, Hartford, Connecticut.

12

13

14

15

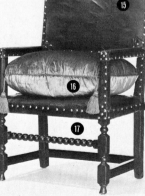

16

Restoration Style, 1660–1700

Comforts and conveniences still known today are introduced in new forms featuring upholstery in couches, side chairs, or armchairs, drawers in tables, chests of drawers or high chests, and tables with hinged leaves supported on gate-legs. Design and decoration of these forms shift radically from rectilinear simplicity at the close of the austere British Commonwealth in 1659 to Baroque curves with restoration of the monarchy and luxury. Innovations in form and decoration reached New England and the Middle Colonies over the late seventeenth century, often influenced the Renaissance Style, and merged into the later William and Mary Style.

Oak is commonly used, but walnut and maple better serve the new fashions. Turnings range from round or oval shapes to discs or spirals. Feet are circular, round or oval. Geometric panels on case furniture or drawers are framed by classical moldings or wide bevels against a field in light and dark woods, black and red paint, or grained patterns.

1. Bevel
2. Boss
3. Ball foot variation
4. Cyma reversa molding
5. Astragal molding
6. Ovolo molding
7. Spiral turning
8. Cleat
9. Split spindle
10. Black paint
11. Pendant or drop
12. Reel turning
13. Recessed seat for cushion
14. Stretchers (front, back, side, medial)
15. Leather upholstery with brass tacks
16. Velvet cushion
17. Ball turning

12. Chest of drawers, Massachusetts, 1660–1690; oak, pine. The Shelburne Museum, Shelburne, Vermont.

13. High chest of drawers, New York, 1680–1700; gumwood. The Metropolitan Museum of Art, Rogers Fund, 1936, New York, New York.

14. Chamber table, Essex County, Massachusetts, 1670–1690; oak. The Art Institute of Chicago, Sewell L. Avery Fund, Chicago, Illinois.

15. Side chair, Philadelphia, Pennsylvania, or Burlington, New Jersey, 1690–1700; walnut. The Philadelphia Museum of Art; purchased by subscription and museum funds, Philadelphia, Pennsylvania.

16. Armchair, Boston, Massachusetts, 1660–1665; oak, maple. The Museum of Fine Arts, Boston, Seth K. Sweetster Fund, Boston, Massachusetts.

William and Mary Style, 1690–1730

Taut curves and crisp rectangles create dynamic tension in the style identified with the English monarch William of Orange and his consort Mary. Case furniture is reduced to crisp planes, and the facade often is decorated with boldly grained walnut or maple veneers, framed by inlaid bands. Classical moldings are exaggerated in size. Baluster-shaped turnings and C-shaped scrolls create rippling movement. Feet usually are round or oval. An alternate foot—known as "Portuguese," paintbrush, or "Spanish"—flares into a scroll. Case furniture may be decorated with imitation lacquer known as japanning, which continues in the Queen Anne and Chippendale styles.

Gate-leg tables and high chests are common forms originating with the Restoration Style. High and narrow backs are upholstered, caned, or, in simple furniture, fitted with spindles turned and split in the manner of the Renaissance Style. Other forms are daybeds, dressing tables repeating the bases of high chests, side tables, easy chairs, and desks with an occasional upper section fitted as a bookcase. Tea tables and tall case clocks are introduced, but are rare.

The Continental Baroque, with a new emphasis on classicism, determined the style. It was encouraged by the king, his Huguenot designer Daniel Marot, and immigrant Dutch and French craftsmen.

17. Armchair, probably New England, 1700–1715; maple, oak. The Henry Francis du Pont Winterthur Museum, Winterthur, Delaware.

18. Table, Massachusetts, 1710–1730; walnut, white pine. The Art Institute of Chicago, gift of Mr. and Mrs. William Salisbury, Chicago, Illinois.

19. Easy chair, probably Ipswich, Massachusetts, 1715–1730; maple. The Museum of Fine Arts, Houston, the Bayou Bend Collection, Houston, Texas.

20. Desk and bookcase, Philadelphia, Pennsylvania, circa 1720; walnut, poplar. The Philadelphia Museum of Art, gift of Mrs. John Wintersteen, Philadelphia, Pennsylvania.

21. Desk (scrutoir), probably Boston, Massachusetts, 1690–1720; walnut, white pine. The Art Institute of Chicago, gift of Joyce Martin Brown, Lena T. Gilbert, Mrs. Harold T. Martin, and Melinda Martin Vance, through the Antiquarian Society, Chicago, Illinois.

22. High chest of drawers, New York, 1690–1725; walnut, Southern yellow pine, cedar. The Art Institute of Chicago, gift of Jamee J. Field and Marshall Field, Chicago, Illinois.

1. Crest with volutes, leaf carving, and C scrolls matches stretcher
2. Finial with ball-over-urn shape
3. Tuscan columnar-turned stile
4. Baluster turning
5. Leather back panel and seat upholstery with brass tacks
6. Stretchers (side, medial, rear)
7. Cyma molding
8. Drawer with knob handle
9. Gate-leg (each side) supports hinged leaf
10. Double baluster turning
11. Spanish, Portuguese, or paintbrush foot
12. Velvet upholstery
13. Horizontally rolled arm
14. Vertically rolled arm support
15. C scroll
16. Medial stretcher with double ball-and-ring turnings
17. Urn-shaped finial
18. Pediment with hood
19. Astragal or bead molding
20. Mirrored glass panel on door (each side)
21. Slide for candlestick (each side)
22. Ball foot
23. Walnut veneer over facade
24. Star, or compass, inlay
25. Herringbone banding
26. Cavetta molding
27. Cyma reversa molding
28. Double astragal or bead molding
29. Flitches of walnut veneer for pattern
30. Pendant or drop
31. Stretchers match skirt shape

23

24

25

26

27

28

Queen Anne Style, 1725–1760

Queen Anne Style curves revolutionize form in cabriole legs, pediments, and aprons, or splats, crests, and arms of chairs. Curves recur in scallop shells carved on legs, chair crest rails, or drawers.

Boston, Newport, New York, and Philadelphia are centers of regional variations. Stretchers occur on chairs, and forms are attenuated in New England. Construction differs; in Philadelphia, for example, chair rails are mortised through the back legs of chairs. New England favors pad feet and Pennsylvania triphid feet. Furniture in Rhode Island, Connecticut, New York, and Pennsylvania occasionally includes slipper and claw-and-ball feet.

Popular forms are rectangular tea tables, gate-leg tables, desks, high chests, dressing tables, and side chairs or easy chairs. Settees, sofas, couches, armchairs, desks and bookcases, and tall clocks are rare. Bedsteads with low posts are common; many occur with high posts, and cabriole legs with pad feet appear on elaborate versions. Tea tables are introduced with a circular tilting top. Card tables occur with a hinged top supported on a gate-leg. Chests of drawers are rare.

The style evolved in Queen Anne's court (1702–1714) and survived to the Revolution. Walnut is popular, cherry and maple are common, and late versions of the style are in mahogany. Japanned decoration in red, green, and gilt usually is on a blue-green field.

23. Bed, Rhode Island, 1735–1750; maple. The Henry Francis du Pont Winterthur Museum, Winterthur, Delaware.

24. Side chair, Rhode Island, 1730–1760; walnut. The Art Institute of Chicago, Robert Allerton Fund, Chicago, Illinois.

25. High chest of drawers; John Pimm, cabinetmaker, with japanning possibly by Thomas Johnson, Boston, Massachusetts, 1740–1750; maple, pine. The Henry Francis du Pont Winterthur Museum, Winterthur, Delaware.

26. Tea table, Connecticut or New York, 1740–1760; cherry. The Yale University Art Gallery, Mabel Brady Garvan Collection, New Haven, Connecticut.

27. Armchair, Philadelphia, Pennsylvania, 1730–1760; walnut. The Art Institute of Chicago, gift of Jessie Spalding Landon, through the Antiquarian Society, Chicago, Illinois.

28. Dressing table, Essex County, Massachusetts, 1750–1770; mahogany, white pine. The Art Institute of Chicago, gift of Mrs. William O. Hunt, Jessie Spalding Landon, Mrs. Harold T. Martin, Adelaide Ryerson, and Melinda Martin Vance, through the Antiquarian Society, Chicago, Illinois.

1. Bedstead (wooden framework)
2. Tester
3. Headboard
4. Columnar footposts
5. Crest rail with yoke (New England type)
6. Curved shoulder (Newport type)
7. Concave, vase-shaped splat and stiles (New England type)
8. Shoe
9. Compass (shape) seat with upholstered slip seat
10. Seat rail with shaped front
11. Cabriole leg
12. Pad foot (mainly New England)
13. Astragal, or bead, molding
14. Chamfered corners
15. Shaped medial and side stretchers (mainly Rhode Island)
16. Scrolled, or broken-arch, pediment
17. Urn-shaped finial (restoration)
18. Carved and gilded scallop shell above festoon
19. Japanned decoration
20. Pendant or drop
21. Paw foot (rare)
22. Applied molding
23. Shaped skirt
24. Pointed slipper foot (mainly Rhode Island and New York)
25. Carved scallop shell (Philadelphia type)
26. Volute
27. Urn-shaped and concave splat
28. Rounded slipper foot with raised tongue
29. Cyma reversa molding
30. Shaped front and side skirts
31. Disc below pad foot

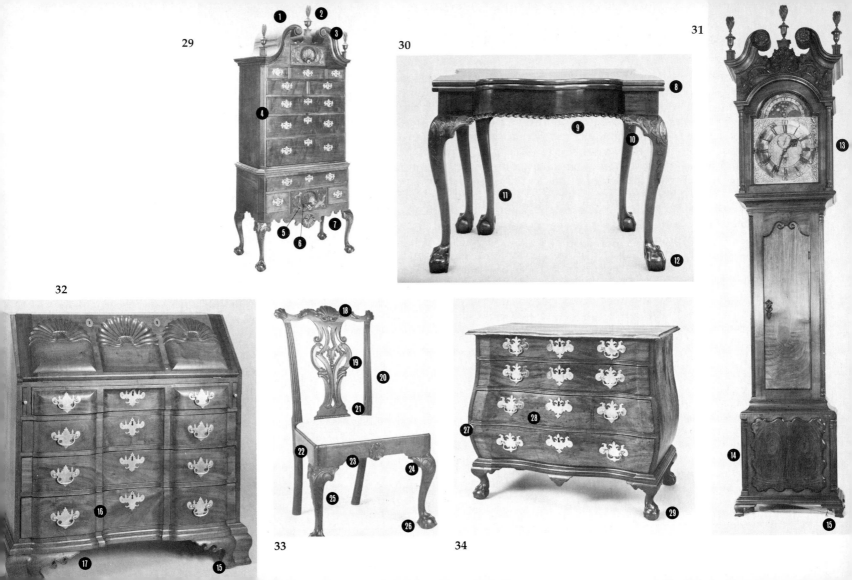

29

30

31

32

33

34

Chippendale Style, 1760–1790

Chinese frets, Gothic arches and quatrefoils, **C**- and **S**-shaped scrolls, ribbons, flowers, leaves, scallop shells, and other French rococo motifs occur with gadrooning, acanthus leaves, columns, capitals, and moldings from Roman architecture. The Chippendale Style is identified today with the English cabinetmaker Thomas Chippendale, whose *Gentleman and Cabinet-Makers Director*—a book of furniture designs published in 1754, 1755, and 1762—nourished the style in England and America.

Mahogany is popular, and walnut, maple, or cherry occur in forms of the Queen Anne Style carved with diverse ornament. Chests of drawers, fire screens, and looking glasses are fashionable. Straight legs replace the cabriole late in the period, ogee bracket feet are popular, and Marlborough feet are favored in Pennsylvania. Japanning is common.

Charleston is a new center of craftsmanship among those continuing from the Queen Anne Style. Regional differences include stretchers on chairs, concave and convex panels known as blocking, and the bombé form in New England. Five legs instead of four occur on card tables in New York, and the shape of claw-and-ball feet varies significantly. Philadelphians make the most elaborate furniture in shops organized in the London manner with specialists.

1. Scrolled, or broken-arch, pediment
2. Finial (Philadelphia type)
3. Rosette
4. Chamfered and fluted corner
5. Rococo leaf carving
6. Scallop shell
7. Shaped apron or skirt
8. Hinged top
9. Applied carved gadrooning
10. "C" scroll
11. Gate-leg (fifth leg: New York only)
12. Claw-and-ball foot (New York type)
13. Fluted Doric column
14. Indented fluted quarter-column
15. Ogee bracket foot
16. Block-front design (New England only)
17. Classical wave pattern
18. Crest rail
19. Splat with lozenge, volutes, and "C" scrolls
20. Fluted stile
21. Shoe
22. Side rail
23. Front rail
24. Bracket
25. Acanthus leaf carving
26. Claw-and-ball foot (Philadelphia type)
27. Bombé form
28. Serpentine curve
29. Claw-and-ball foot (Massachusetts type)

29. High chest of drawers, probably Maryland, 1755–1790; mahogany, yellow pine, poplar, cedar. The Art Institute of Chicago, gift of the Antiquarian Society, Chicago, Illinois.

30. Gaming table, New York, 1755–1790; mahogany, poplar, oak. The Art Institute of Chicago, gift of Robert Allerton, Bessie Bennett, Mr. and Mrs. Robert Brown, Annie Dunlap Estate, in memory of Annie Wisner, and Mrs. Potter Palmer, Chicago, Illinois.

31. Clock, Philadelphia, Pennsylvania, 1755–1790; Greenfield Village and Henry Ford Museum, Dearborn, Michigan.

32. Desk, probably Norwich, Connecticut, 1755–1805; mahogany, white pine. The Art Institute of Chicago, gift of Jessie Spalding Landon, through the Antiquarian Society, Chicago, Illinois.

33. Side chair, Philadelphia, Pennsylvania, 1755–1765; mahogany. The Art Institute of Chicago, gift of the Robert R. McCormick Charitable Trust, Chicago, Illinois.

34. Chest of drawers, Boston, Massachusetts, 1770–1795; mahogany, white pine. The Art Institute of Chicago, the Helen Bowen Blair Fund, Chicago, Illinois.

35

36

37

38

39

40

Federal Style, 1790–1815

Forms of mahogany veneered with contrasting mahogany, maple, birch, or satinwood are severe, with straight, oval, and serpentine lines. Decoration is inlaid or carved. Occasionally it is painted. Motifs are Roman bellflowers, paterae, urns, festoons, flutes, acanthus leaves, and pilasters with such contemporary elements as shields, Prince of Wales feathers, or eagles representative of both Rome and the new nation. Rococo curves, flowers, and ribbons or Gothic arches and quatrefoils occasionally appear. Accents are inlaid lines or bands. Straight legs taper in planes or are circular in cross-section with reeding. Feet often are bulbous turnings or tapered spades.

Forms of the Chippendale Style continue in the Federal with new delicacy. They include stands, card tables, dining tables, and Pembroke tables. Sofas, settees, and chairs occur in great variety. Sideboards and sewing tables are introduced.

Robert Adam originated the English style during the 1760s, and it reached the United States by 1790. Influential English books are Alice Hepplewhite's *Cabinet-Maker and Upholsterer's Drawing Book,* published in parts from 1791 to 1794, and other guides for English craftsmen. Local variations are pronounced in form and decoration.

1. Shield-shaped back
2. Carved drapery festoon
3. Urn
4. Spade foot
5. Serpentine shape
6. Inlaid flutes
7. Inlaid patera
8. Inlaid husks
9. Inlaid urn
10. Stringing (inlaid bands)
11. Finial
12. Mullion
13. Inlaid pilaster
14. Birch veneer
15. Hinged top
16. Carved basket of flowers
17. Reeding
18. Maple veneer

35. Side chair, carving attributed to Samuel McIntire, Salem, Massachusetts, 1795–1811; mahogany. The Art Institute of Chicago, gift of Edith Almy Adams through the Antiquarian Society, Chicago, Illinois.

36. Sideboard, New York City area, 1790–1815; mahogany, white pine, poplar, oak. The Art Institute of Chicago, gift of Mrs. Clive Runnells, through the Antiquarian Society, Chicago, Illinois.

37. Pembroke table, New York City area, 1795–1810; mahogany. The Art Institute of Chicago, gift of the Illinois District Chapter of the American Institute of Interior Designers and Emily Crane Chadbourne, Chicago, Illinois.

38. Desk and bookcase, New Hampshire, 1800–1815; mahogany and birch veneers, white pine. The Art Institute of Chicago, gift of Mr. and Mrs. Robert Sack, Chicago, Illinois.

39. Card table, Salem, Massachusetts, 1800–1815; mahogany, white pine. The Art Institute of Chicago, gift of Jessie Spalding Landon, through the Antiquarian Society, Chicago, Illinois.

40. Chest of drawers and dressing glass, Boston, Massachusetts, 1800–1810; mahogany, white pine. The Art Institute of Chicago, anonymous gift, Chicago, Illinois.

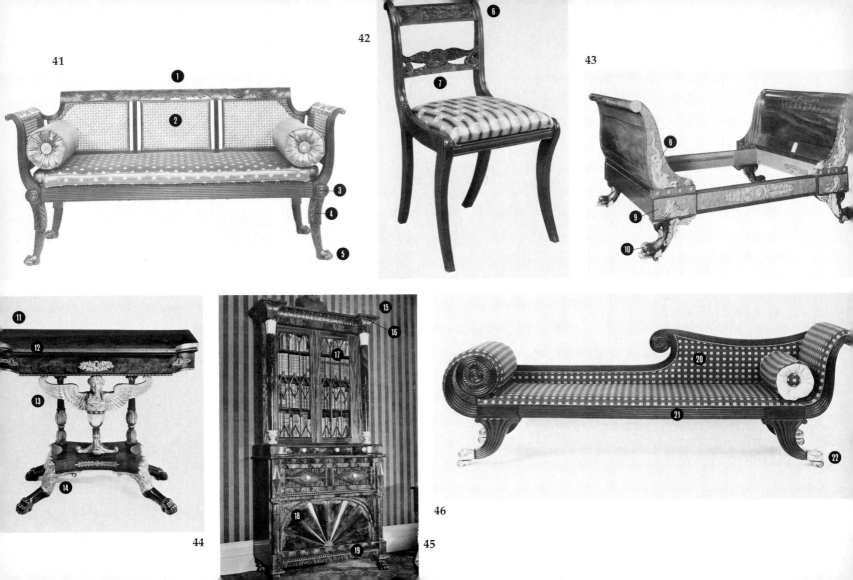

41

42

43

44

46

45

Classical Styles, 1805–1830

Dog or lion feet, anthemia, and other motifs with adaptations in form of couches and *klismos* chairs revive the classical world with a Grecian emphasis.

Sofa tables, parlor tables, and wardrobes are new forms. New designs appear for beds, card tables, sideboards, and sofas.

Carved decoration in the principal wood of mahogany often is painted black or gilded. Inlaid lines may occur in ebony and veneers in maple. Ormolu is common and imitated with gilt stenciling.

The American eagle is among occasional motifs. Other motifs from Egyptian art are popularized by Napoleon's campaigns and Nelson's victories. Gothic influence occurs in pointed arches and quatrefoils.

Diverse designs reveal the continuity of English influence and a direct relationship with France. Significant English publications are cabinetmakers' guides, Thomas Hope's *Household Furniture* of 1807, George Smith's *Household Furniture* of 1808, and Rudolph Ackermann's *Repository of Arts*. Influential French publications are Pierre de la Mesangere's *Collections des muebles et objets de goût* and the 1801 and 1812 editions of Charles Percier and Pierre F. L. Fontaine's *Recuil de decorations intérieures*.

New York City becomes the center of fashion and furniture production. Regional variations occur in Boston, Philadelphia, and Baltimore.

1. **Carved cornucopia**
2. **Caning**
3. **Carved lion face**
4. **Carved water-leaf**
5. **Lion foot**
6. ***Klismos* chair adaptation**
7. **Eagle-shaped splat**
8. **Ormolu**
9. **Satinwood veneer**
10. **Dolphin foot**
11. **Hinged top**
12. **Brass inlay**
13. **Sphinx**
14. **Gilt wood**
15. **Cornice**
16. **Acanthus leaf**
17. **Gothic (pointed) arch mullion**
18. **Anthemion**
19. **Gadrooning**
20. **Haircloth upholstery**
21. **Reeding**
22. **Castor with eagle design**

41. Settee, Phyfe Style, New York City, 1810–1820; mahogany. The Art Institute of Chicago, Robert Allerton Fund, Chicago, Illinois.

42. Side chair, New York City, 1810–1820; mahogany. The Art Institute of Chicago, gift of Emily Crane Chadbourne, Chicago, Illinois.

43. Bedstead, Charles-Honoré Lannuier, New York City, circa 1817; mahogany with satinwood veneer. The Albany Institute of History and Art, gift of Mrs. William Dexter, Albany, New York.

44. Card table, Charles-Honoré Lannuier, New York City, circa 1817; mahogany. The Albany Institute of History and Art, gift of Stephen Van Rensselaer Crosby, Albany, New York.

45. Desk and bookcase, Antoine Gabriel Quervelle, Philadelphia, Pennsylvania, circa 1835; mahogany. The Munson-Williams-Proctor Institute, Utica, New York.

46. Grecian couch, New England, 1810–1835; mahogany, birch, white pine. The Art Institute of Chicago, gift of Joseph P. Antonow, Chicago, Illinois.

French Restauration Style, 1830–1850

Simplicity, practicality, and comfort mark the French Restauration Style. Born in France, it evolved during restoration of the Bourbons to the throne, from 1814 to 1848. Undulating curves balance geometric forms. Plain surfaces are relieved by spare ornament. The style includes the Egyptian lotus, circles, ormolu, and such simple moldings as the astragal, or bead. White marble and particularly the rich color and grain of mahogany veneers are significant to this style.

Forms often are conservative versions of the late Classical Style. Card tables retain the single pedestal, sofas an asymmetrical shape, and stools the curule form. Chairs are inspired by the *klismos* shape in Classical Greece, but they typically are transformed by curves in the crest, urn-shaped splats, braces curved from crest to seat, and the shape of legs.

Simplicity of the French Restauration Style encouraged interpretations over a long period in large and small centers of craftsmanship from Boston to New Orleans. Pierre de la Mésangère's Parisian periodical *Collection de meubles et objets de goût* recorded the style in France; George Smith's *Cabinet-Maker and Upholsterer's Guide*, published in 1826 in London, offered the English variation; and John Hall's *The Cabinet Makers Assistant*, published in 1840 in Baltimore, recorded a version in the United States.

1. Curved and concave crest rail
2. Urn-shaped splat
3. Cabriole leg
4. Hinged top
5. Central pedestal support
6. Red leather upholstery
7. Ormolu
8. Linen and wool rep upholstery
9. Mahogany veneer
10. Concentric circle motif
11. Marble top
12. Mirror
13. Canted corner

47. Side chair (*chaise gondole*), probably New Orleans, Louisiana, 1835–1850; mahogany. The Museum of Fine Arts, Houston, the Bayou Bend Collection, Houston, Texas.

48. Card table, New York City, 1835–1845; mahogany. The New-York Historical Society, New York, New York.

49. Library chair, probably New York City, 1830–1840; mahogany. Sleepy Hollow Restorations, Sunnyside, Tarrytown, New York.

50. Daybed (*méridienne*), attributed to Duncan Phyfe, New York City, 1837; mahogany. The Metropolitan Museum of Art, L. E. Katzenbach Foundation gift, 1966, New York, New York.

51. Pier table, attributed to Duncan Phyfe, New York City, 1830–1840; mahogany with marble top. The Metropolitan Museum of Art, Edgar J. Kauffmann, Jr., Charitable Foundation Fund, 1968, New York, New York.

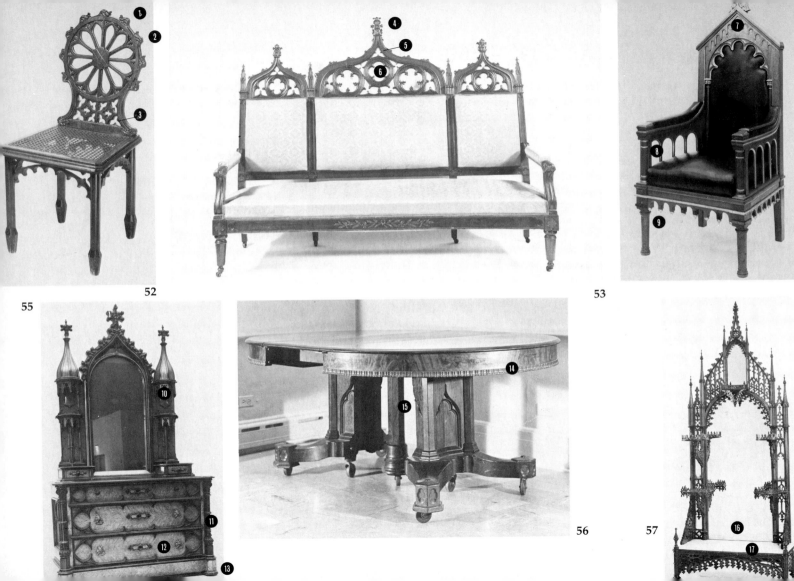

52

53

54

55

56

57

Gothic Revival Style, 1840–1860

Pointed arches, trefoils, quatrefoils, tracery, crockets, Tudor roses, and clustered columns from the architectural style common in western Europe between the twelfth and the sixteenth centuries are adapted to mid-nineteenth-century furniture forms. Among them, the étagère, or whatnot, and dining tables extended by mechanical parts are newly popular.

Medieval furniture forms are not reproduced. They were generally unrecognized in a period of vague historical knowledge, and those known did not meet the comforts and needs of contemporary life.

Walnut and oak are common woods, with occasional use of mahogany and rosewood. Furniture ranges from large in scale to small; silhouettes are bold; and carved details accent plain surfaces.

English fashion inspired the Gothic Revival Style. It never gained the popularity it held abroad, but the motifs had been a consistent theme since the mid-eighteenth-century Chippendale Style.

Contemporaries also knew the Gothic Revival Style as *Norman* and *Medieval*. Motifs mingle with those of the Restauration Style in an early phase and later with motifs of the Rococo Revival Style. Significant books offering designs are A. W. Pugin's *Gothic Furniture in the Style of the Fifteenth Century*, published in London in 1835, and Robert Conner's *Cabinet Makers Assistant*, published in New York City in 1842.

1. **Wheel-shaped back**
2. **Crocket**
3. **Trefoil**
4. **Finial**
5. **Ogee arch**
6. **Quatrefoil**
7. **Lancet arch**
8. **Roman arch**
9. **Pendant or drop**
10. **Trefoil arch**
11. **Cluster column**
12. **Maple veneer**
13. **Plinth**
14. **Machine banding**
15. **Octagonal column**
16. **Mirror**
17. **Marble** .

52. Side chair, designed by Alexander Jackson Davis, probably 1841, made by Richard Byrne, Dobbs Ferry, New York, or Ambrose Wright, Hastings (now Hastings-on-Hudson), New York, circa 1842; oak. Lyndhurst; a property of the National Trust for Historic Preservation, Tarrytown, New York.

53. Settee, attributed to Thomas Brooks, Brooklyn, New York, circa 1846; walnut, cherry. The Society for the Preservation of New England Antiquities, Boston, Massachusetts.

54. Armchair, design attributed to James Renwick, Jr., Washington, D.C., 1846–1855; walnut. The Smithsonian Institution, Furnishings Collection, Washington, D.C.

55. Chest of drawers and mirror, United States, circa 1846–1866; walnut, maple. The Smithsonian Institution, the National Museum of History and Technology, Washington, D.C., gift of the city of Bridgeport, Connecticut.

56. Extension dining table, New York City, 1842–1845; mahogany. The Munson-Williams-Proctor Institute, gift of Mrs. Erving Pruyn, Utica, New York.

57. Étagère, probably New York City, 1845–1855; rosewood with marble top. The Brooklyn Museum, H. Randolph Lever Fund, New York, New York.

58

59

60

61

62

Elizabethan Style,   1850–1915

Ball and spiral turnings, strapwork, and flowers with leaves are features of the Elizabethan Style. Less popular in America than in England, it is mainly confined in the United States to chairs in walnut, mahogany, or rosewood, and to informal painted bedroom suites known as "cottage furniture."

The period of greatest popularity was at mid-century. Vague historical knowledge wrongly credited motifs and chairs with high backs to the reign of Queen Elizabeth, instead of correctly assigning them to the Restoration and the William and Mary styles of England.

The Elizabethan Style frequently mingled with the contemporary Rococo Revival and is a variant of the Renaissance Revival Style, based on English instead of continental sources. It lingered through the late nineteenth and early twentieth centuries as an accent for rooms furnished in other styles.

Walter Scott's novels during the 1820s influenced concern for the "Elizabethan" period, as did Henry Shaw's investigation of English antique furniture titled *Specimens of Ancient Furniture,* published in London in 1836. Robert Bridgen's influential designs for this style appeared in his *Furniture with Candelabra and Interior Decoration,* published in London in 1838.

1. **Spiral turning**
2. **Needlework upholstery**
3. **Baluster turning**
4. **Castor**
5. **Split spindle**
6. **Adaptation of strapwork design**
7. **Ball turning**
8. **Stretchers (front, back, side, medial)**

58. Side chair, United States, 1840–1860; walnut. Greenfield Village and Henry Ford Museum, Dearborn, Michigan.

59. Chest of drawers and mirror, probably New York City, circa 1850; painted pine. Sleepy Hollow Restorations, Sunnyside, Tarrytown, New York.

60. Side chair, probably New York City, circa 1851–1861; rosewood, mahogany. The Museum of the City of New York, gift of Mrs. Henry De Bevoise Schenck, New York, New York.

61. Armchair, United States, 1850–1860; mahogany. The Stowe-Day Foundation, Hartford, Connecticut.

62. Armchair, United States, 1890–1900; mahogany. The Brooklyn Museum, New York, New York.

63

64

65

66

67

Rococo Revival Style, 1845–1870

Curves in **C** or **S** shapes are the basis of furniture form. In the Rococo Revival Style, they mingle in decoration with scallop shells, leaves, flowers—especially the rose—baskets of flowers, the acanthus, and the cabochon. Legs are cabriole in form and often terminate in scroll feet. Contemporaries knew this style as the *Louis Quatorze*, the *Louis Quinze*, or the *Antique French*.

Rococo taste in the court of Louis XV was the main precedent. Craftsmen made some reproductions, but form and decoration also ranged from French furniture of the late seventeenth century to the mid-eighteenth. Motifs are combined and boldly reinterpreted from original delicacy. Side tables, sofas, chairs, and other eighteenth-century forms are extended with the "tête-à-tête," chairs with curved backs, and the étagère, or whatnot, for displaying objects.

Sources dictated walnut and painted woods. Rosewood and mahogany are common. Woods are laminated, as in the Naturalistic Style, to achieve delicate designs.

The revival emerged in England and France during the 1820s, became a movement by the 1840s, and reigned in America during the 1850s. Designers often combined the cabriole leg and motifs with the Naturalistic Style. Features survived in mass-produced furniture into the 1880s.

1. Cartouche
2. **C** scroll
3. **S** scroll
4. Mirror
5. Console
6. Serpentine curve
7. Scallop shell
8. Rose flower and leaves
9. Cabriole leg
10. Acanthus leaf
11. Silk damask upholstery
12. Scroll foot
13. Marble top
14. Classical woman's head (mask)
15. Diaper-incised design
16. Apron or skirt
17. Basket of flowers

63. Étagère, New York City, 1850–1860; rosewood with marble top. The Newark Museum, Newark, New Jersey, gift of the Museum of the City of New York.

64. Étagère, New York City, 1850–1870; rosewood with marble top. The Art Institute of Chicago, Elizabeth R. Vaughan Fund, Chicago, Illinois.

65. Side chair, New York City, 1845–1855; painted and gilt mahogany. The New York State Museum, Albany, New York.

66. Pier mirror, United States, circa 1853; gilt wood. The Metropolitan Museum of Art, gift of Mrs. Frederick Wildman, 1964, New York, New York.

67. Pier table, attributed to Alexander Roux, New York City, 1850–1860; rosewood. The Museum of the City of New York, gift of the Estate of Harold Wilmerding Bell, New York, New York.

68

69

70

71

Naturalistic Style, 1850–1865

Fruit and flowers as well as leaves of the grape, oak, or rose are prominent in the Naturalistic Style. Carving is realistic, in contrast to generalization in the eighteenth century.

The style frequently merges with the contemporary Rococo Revival Style. Forms are identical and scrolls in **C** and **S** shapes, scallop shells, and the cabochon mingle with the motifs from nature.

Designs often are accomplished with a lamination process. Several layers of wood, each one-sixteenth of an inch thick, are glued together with the grain at right angles. Layers vary from three to sixteen, the average being six to eight. Panels are steamed in molds for undulating forms of such strength that a tracery of motifs could be carved into the backs of sofas and chairs or the skirts of tables. Superimposed carved elements increase the three-dimensional effect. Mahogany, walnut, and rosewood are favored as surface woods.

The style evolved with the English Rococo Revival during the 1820s. It assumed an original character in the United States through intricate carving integrated with form.

1. **C** scroll
2. **S** scroll
3. **Putti (head of winged child)**
4. **Oak leaves with acorns**
5. **Serpentine curve in laminated rosewood**
6. **Grapes and grape leaves**
7. **Silk damask upholstery**
8. **Marble top**
9. **Rose flowers and leaves**
10. **Cabriole leg**
11. **Basket of flowers**

68. Bed, John Henry Belter, New York City, 1850–1860; laminated rosewood. The Brooklyn Museum, gift of Mrs. Ernest Vietor, New York, New York.

69. Side chair, New York City, 1850–1867; laminated rosewood. The Art Institute of Chicago, gift of Gloria and Richard Manney.

70. Center table, John Henry Belter, New York City, 1856–1861; rosewood with marble top. The Museum of the City of New York, gift of Mr. and Mrs. Gunther Vieter, New York, New York.

71. Sofa, New York City, 1850–1860; laminated rosewood. The Art Institute of Chicago, gift of Mrs. Anne McCall Dommerich, Mrs. Margaret McCall Dommerich, Mrs. Esther Foote, and Mrs. Charlotte McCall Ladd, in memory of Mr. and Mrs. Sumner T. McCall, Chicago, Illinois.

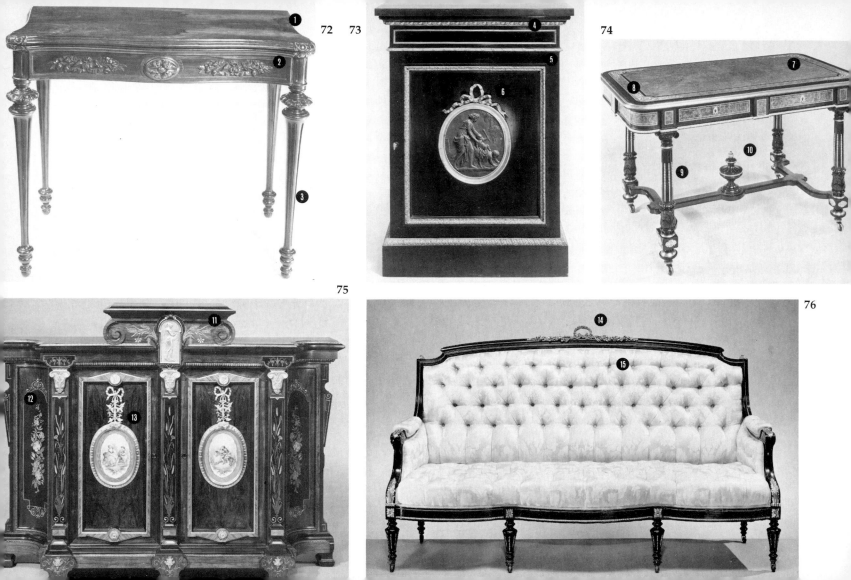

72 73 74

75 76

Louis XVI Style, 1850–1914

Rectangular shapes are contrasted with ovals and arches, straight and tapered legs are fluted, and plain surfaces are accented with classical moldings, columns, wreaths, garlands, urns, lyres, acanthus, and beading. The Louis XVI Style is the only revival in the mid-nineteenth century of an earlier period in form as well as decoration. But the revival is identified by bolder design and differences in craftsmanship and woods.

The long period of popularity includes many variations. They range from an initial period of exaggerated motifs in the 1850s and their close imitation in the 1860s to novel adaptations through the period.

Costly materials and elaborate workmanship are characteristic. Rosewood or ebonized woods are favored in the earliest versions. Walnut occurs with the 1890s. Dark woods contrast with gilt metal mounts, elaborate marquetry, panels of light woods, ivory inlays, and porcelain plaques. Carving is featured during the 1850s.

The English and the French originated this style. Eugenie, consort to Napoleon III, endorsed and popularized it after 1853, when it became known by the alternate name of the "Marie Antoinette" Style. The straight leg and motifs often are adapted to forms of the Renaissance Revival and Neo-Greek styles.

1. Hinged top
2. Floral and ribbon carving
3. Tapered and fluted leg
4. Classical egg-and-dart motif
5. Ebonized maple
6. Ceramic plaque with ormolu frame
7. Amboina veneer
8. Ivory inlay
9. Ionic column with ormolu
10. Medial stretcher with urn
11. Incised gilt decoration
12. Marquetry
13. Porcelain plaque with ormolu frame
14. Ormolu
15. Silk damask upholstery

72. Card table, Alexander Roux, New York City, 1850–1857; rosewood. The Brooklyn Museum, H. Randolph Lever Fund, New York, New York.

73. Cabinet (one of a pair), Leon Marcotte, New York City, circa 1860; ebonized maple with ormolu, ceramic plaque, and gilt moldings. The Metropolitan Museum of Art, gift of Mrs. Chester D. Noyes, 1968, New York, New York.

74. Library table, Leon Marcotte, New York city, 1862–1872; amboina with hornbeam, ivory inlay, and gilt metal mounts. The Metropolitan Museum of Art, gift of Mrs. Robert W. de Forest, 1934, New York, New York.

75. Cabinet, Alexander Roux, New York City, 1866; rosewood with porcelain plaques and gilt mounts. The Metropolitan Museum of Art, Edgar J. Kauffmann, Jr., Charitable Foundation Fund, 1968, New York, New York.

76. Sofa, Leon Marcotte, New York City, circa 1860; ebonized maple with gilt mounts. The Metropolitan Museum of Art, gift of Mrs. Chester D. Noyes, 1968, New York, New York.

Renaissance Revival Style, 1850–1880

Renaissance, Baroque, and mannerist approaches to design, especially in sixteenth- and seventeenth-century France, are combined in a period of vague historical knowledge to inspire the bold Renaissance Revival Style enduring through freedom of interpretation. Variations range from florid and curvilinear during the 1850s to severe and angular by the 1870s. Form enters the revival in the 1890s and survives to the 1920s. The Elizabethan Style is a variant based on English rather than French sources.

Common motifs are flowers, fruit, game, classical busts, bizarre faces known as "masks," acanthus scrolls, strapwork, and tassels. They are carved in high relief, and many recur in porcelain or marquetry insets on case furniture and table tops. Significant architectural motifs adapted to furniture are pediments, pilasters, columns, balusters, brackets, and volutes.

This style often merges in form and decoration with others. Cabriole legs and other elements of the Rococo Revival appear in the 1850s. They tend to disappear in the 1860s before straight legs and motifs from the Louis XVI Style. Common by the 1870s are anthemia and other ornaments of the Neo-Greek Style or the cloven hoof associated with it and the Egyptian Revival.

Mahogany and walnut are favored woods. Rosewood and ebony are occasional. Burled walnut panels are featured by the 1870s. Upholstery, especially in chairs, is prominent.

1. Grotesque mask
2. Acanthus scroll
3. Silk damask upholstery
4. Rococo Revival skirt and cabriole leg
5. Strapwork adaptation
6. Carved floral bouquet in urn
7. Adaptation of cluster column
8. Carved tassel
9. Classical woman's head (mask)
10. Louis XVI Revival leg
11. Console
12. Mirror
13. Baluster adaptation
14. Ball-foot adaptation

77. Sofa, New York City, 1850–1865; laminated mahogany. The Art Institute of Chicago, gift of Mr. and Mrs. Louis J. Fischer, Chicago, Illinois.

78. Piano, Robert Nunns and John Clark, New York City, 1851; rosewood. The Metropolitan Museum of Art, gift of George Lowther, 1906, New York, New York.

79. Armchair, John Jellif, Newark, New Jersey, 1860–1870; rosewood. The Newark Museum, gift of Mrs. John Laimbeer, Jr., Newark, New Jersey.

80. Étagère, Julius Dessoir, New York City, 1855–1865; rosewood. The Metropolitan Museum of Art, Anonymous Gift Fund, 1969, New York, New York.

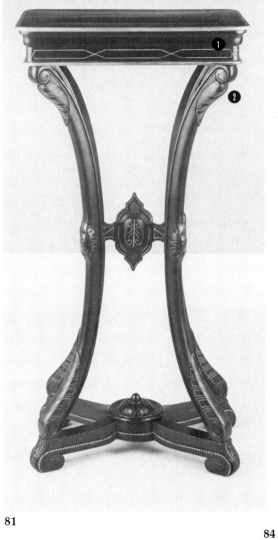

81

82

83

85

84

Neo-Greek Style, 1855–1885

Curved and rectangular elements boldly contrast in shapes. Common motifs from ancient Greek architecture and ornament are pilasters, columns, flutes, acroteria, foliate scrolls, anthemia, and the Greek key design. They are carved in high relief, inlaid in contrasting light and dark woods, or incised and gilded.

The alternate names of "New" and "Modern" Greek identify a different interpretation of sources than in the earlier Classical Style. Motifs are exaggerated in size, changed in proportion, and combined in new ways. Taut curves and crisp angles are tensely balanced. The shapes of the Greek curule and *klismos* chairs are revived. Feet vary from the cloven hoof to scrolls. Case furniture often rests on a high plinth.

The French originated the Neo-Greek Style. It reached the United States in the late 1850s, became popular by the 1870s, and influenced factory furniture in the 1880s. Motifs often merge with the contemporary Louis XVI and Renaissance Revival styles.

1. Incised gilt lines
2. Anthemion
3. Boss
4. Fluted pilaster
5. Lion head
6. Greek curule shape
7. Burl walnut panel
8. Greek key design
9. Metal plaque
10. Plinth

81. Stand, New York City, circa 1870; ebonized cherry. The Metropolitan Museum of Art, Edgar J. Kauffmann, Jr., Charitable Foundation Fund, 1968, New York, New York.

82. Armchair, New York City, 1860–1870; ebonized walnut. The Brooklyn Museum, gift of Sarah Fanning Chapman and Bertha Fanning Taylor, New York, New York.

83. Bedstead, Nelson, Matter, and Company, Grand Rapids, Michigan, 1870–1880; walnut. The Margaret Woodbury Strong Museum, gift of

Mr. and Mrs. John C. Doolittle, Rochester, New York.

84. Stool, Alexander Roux, New York City, circa 1865; painted woods. The Metropolitan Museum of Art, Edgar J. Kauffmann, Jr., Charitable Foundation Fund, 1969, New York, New York.

85. Music cabinet, George Croome, Boston, Massachusetts, 1875–1877; mahogany, rosewood. The Art Institute of Chicago, Elizabeth R. Vaughan Fund, Chicago, Illinois.

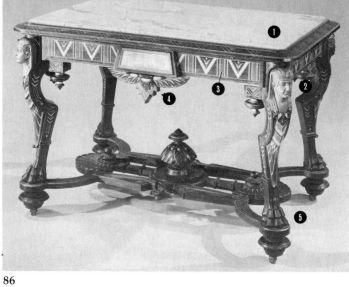

86

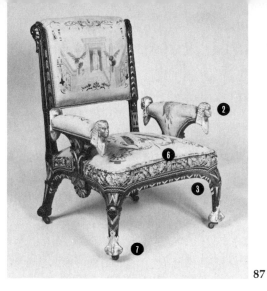

87

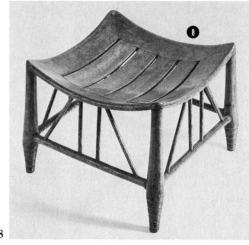

88

89

Egyptian Revival Style, 1865–1890

Sphynx heads, clustered columns, lotus capitals, winged orbs, zigzag lines, palmettes, the cloven hoof, and paw-shaped feet are Egyptian motifs emerging as occasional motifs early in the nineteenth century and combined with others late in the century for the Egyptian Revival Style. Popularity is limited.

Tables, chairs, stands, and stools mainly are common forms of the late nineteenth century with motifs adapted to them. The Egyptian stool with a concave seat and turned stretchers and legs is the principal revival of an ancient form.

Treatment of motifs may show contrasting elements, even on a single piece of furniture, from shallow relief to three-dimensional exuberance. Gilt decoration is common against dark and often ebonized woods. Exotic combinations of materials include woods, marble, and gilt bronze.

English fashion encouraged the Egyptian Style. Monuments or artifacts in tombs from about 2,700 B.C. to about 1,000 B.C. are the main source for motifs. Exhibition of Egyptian antiquities in the international exposition at London in 1862, completion of the Suez Canal in 1869, and British concern with Egyptian affairs after 1876 all stimulated interest in Egypt and Egyptian art.

1. Marble top
2. Sphinx head
3. Gilt incised ornament
4. Winged orb
5. Lion-paw feet
6. Tapestry upholstery
7. Claw-and-ball foot
8. Egyptian stool form
9. Lotus capital
10. Cluster column

86. Center table, New York City, 1870–1880; rosewood, marble. The Metropolitan Museum of Art, Edgar J. Kauffmann, Jr., Charitable Foundation Fund, 1968, New York, New York.

87. Armchair, New York City, 1870–1880; rosewood, gilt metal. The Art Institute of Chicago, gift of Suzanne Waller Worthy, Chicago, Illinois.

88. Stool, United States, 1870–1880; oak. The Newark Museum, bequest of Susan Dwight Bliss, Newark, New Jersey.

89. Stool, United States, 1870–1880; maple painted black. The Metropolitan Museum of Art, Rogers Fund, 1967, New York, New York.

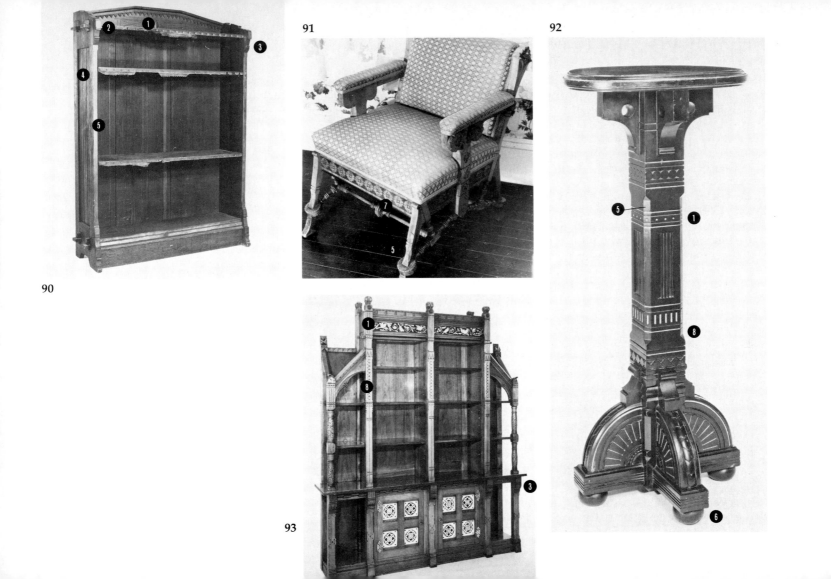

90

91

92

93

Eastlake Style, 1870–1890

Charles Locke Eastlake was chagrined that Americans associated his name with shoddy, mass-produced furniture superficially inspired by simple English Medieval, Renaissance, and eighteenth-century furniture he endorsed for sound construction, practical form, and generalized decoration. Features of the Eastlake Style are rectangular forms in oak or cherry, with brackets, trestles, and machined decoration of grooves, chamfers, geometric ornament, and spindles. The style evolved during the 1870s and merges in factories with Neo-Greek and Renaissance Revival styles.

Eastlake became known through his *Hints on Household Taste*, published in London in 1868. Developed from magazine articles, the book reached nine American editions from 1872 to 1890. Eastlake endorses relationships between form, function, and craftsmanship, approves carving or inlay by hand, condemns machines for imitating handcraftsmanship, and endorsed machines for furniture meeting his standards.

Eastlake differed from William Morris and other English contemporaries concerned with reforming awkward shapes, abundant ornament, or careless craftsmanship. They relied on medieval standards. Eastlake emphasized principles evident in many periods, including his own.

Art Furniture and Arts and Crafts furniture often suggest Eastlake's philosophy. Both include motifs reducing his concepts to a style.

1. Incised lines
2. Triangle motif
3. Bracket
4. Grooves
5. Chamfer
6. Ball foot
7. Stylized flower
8. Geometric ornament

90. Bookcase, William Homes Company, Boston, Massachusetts, circa 1876; oak. The Hudson River Museum, gift of the Doran Family, Yonkers, New York.

91. Armchair, New York City, circa 1876; maple. Sagamore Hill, National Historic Site, Oyster Bay, New York.

92. Pedestal, probably New York City, 1870–1880; ebonized cherry. The Metropolitan Museum of Art, Edgar J. Kauffmann, Jr., Charitable Foundation Fund, 1969, New York, New York.

93. Bookcase, Isaac E. Scott, Chicago, Illinois, 1875; walnut. The Chicago Architecture Foundation, Chicago, Illinois.

94

95

96

97

98

Art Furniture Styles, 1880–1914

"Art" is vaguely linked to "Furniture" in an English trend toward new directions in design, craftsmanship, and ornament. Approaches vary from adaptations of the English Queen Anne mode of the 1880s to those published in London in 1887 in *Art Furniture Designed by Edward W. Godwin F.S.A. and Others, with Hints and Suggestions on Domestic Furniture and Decoration by William Watt.* The movement was popular into the 1890s and lingered to 1914.

Forms vary from simple to complex. Planes and angularity among some designers contrast with curves among others.

Ornament is diverse. It includes classical moldings, medieval spindles, and spiral turnings of the Restoration Style. Other sources range from oriental to Near Eastern, from Moorish to Egyptian. Japanese art received particular emphasis. It contributed the principle of asymmetrical composition, in such forms as cupboards or the arrangement of motifs, and encouraged stylized, two-dimensional designs. Decoration is achieved by shallow carving, marquetry, or inlaid woods and metals.

Woods vary. Some are stained black, to suggest ebony and lacquer. Bamboo is imported, and imitations in maple repeat a motif in the Windsor Style of the late eighteenth and early nineteenth centuries.

1. Mirror
2. Ionic column
3. Spiral-turned baluster
4. Glass door
5. Chinese fret
6. Turned spindles
7. Chinese bracket foot
8. Ebonized finish
9. Marquetry of cherry blossoms
10. Incised lines
11. Carved panel of stylized flowers
12. Silk damask upholstery
13. Brass inlay
14. Relief carving
15. Reeded leg
16. Glass-ball foot
17. Bamboo turnings

94. Cabinet, Charles Tisch, New York City, 1884; rosewood. The Metropolitan Museum of Art, gift of Charles Tisch, 1889, New York, New York.

95. Side chair, Herter Brothers, New York City, 1870–1880; ebonized cherry. The Art Institute of Chicago, Mrs. Alfred S. Burdick Fund, Chicago, Illinois.

96. Clock, George Grant Elmslie and William Purcell, designers, Chicago, Illinois, 1912; mahogany with brass and wood inlays. The Art Institute of Chicago, gift of Mrs. Theodore D. Tiecken, Chicago, Illinois.

97. Armchair, Tiffany Studios, New York City, 1890; unidentified wood. The Shelburne Museum, Shelburne, Vermont.

98. Bedstead, probably New York City, 1875–1885; maple. The Metropolitan Museum of Art, Edgar J. Kauffmann, Jr., Charitable Foundation Fund, 1968, New York, New York.

99

100

101

102

103

104

Arts and Crafts Styles, 1895–1915

Handcraftsmanship, or its appearance, is a theme among individualistic approaches to furniture that is generally identified in America with the Arts and Crafts movement. Furniture usually is rectilinear and often offers a relationship between form and function. Ornament among different designers is oriental, medieval, Renaissance, Gothic, or Art Nouveau in inspiration.

The Arts and Crafts movement evolved from British opinion that machines were lowering standards of form, decoration, and craftsmanship. Various efforts combining reform of the arts with reform of industrial society reached America, with diverse results. The principal themes are William Morris's emphasis on medieval art, E. W. Godwin's solutions in the Art Furniture movement, and Charles Locke Eastlake's principles.

Solutions are individual, but the movement is national. Innovative architects in Illinois, encouraged by Frank Lloyd Wright, and in California by Charles and Henry Greene, designed furniture sympathetic with their buildings. George Niedecken in the Midwest, Lucia K. Mathews and Arthur F. Mathews on the West Coast, and Elbert Hubbard, with the brothers Gustav, Leopold, and J. George Stickley on the East Coast are among the diverse contributors to the movement.

Oak is a common wood. The use of it is a revival of an English and American material from the Medieval and Renaissance styles.

1. **Applied bands**
2. **Ogee, or cyma recta, molding**
3. **Leather upholstery**
4. **Carved and painted panel**
5. **Gothic trefoil adaptation**
6. **Ebony pegs**
7. **Relief carving of Japanese designs**
8. **Pewter and copper inlays**

99. Desk, Niedecken Walbridge Company, Milwaukee, Wisconsin, circa 1910; oak. The Art Institute of Chicago, gift of the Graham Foundation for Advanced Studies in the Fine Arts, Chicago, Illinois.

100. Side chair, Frank Lloyd Wright Firm, Chicago, Illinois, 1904; oak. The Art Institute of Chicago, Bessie Bennett Fund, Chicago, Illinois.

101. Desk, Lucia K. Mathews and Arthur F. Mathews, San Francisco, California, 1906–1918; walnut. The Oakland Museum Association, gift of the Art Guild, Oakland, California.

102. Side chair, George Grant Elmslie, designer, Chicago, Illinois, circa 1910; oak. The Art Institute of Chicago, gift of the Antiquarian Society, through Mrs. William P. Boggess II, Chicago, Illinois.

103. Chest of drawers and mirror, Charles Greene, designer, Pasadena, California, 1908; walnut. The Gamble House, Greene and Greene Museum and Library, Pasadena, California; photograph by Marvin Rand.

104. Rocking chair, Harvey Ellis, designer for Gustav Stickley, Eastwood, New York, 1903; oak with pewter and copper inlays. The Art Institute of Chicago, gift of Mrs. Sidney Haskins, Chicago, Illinois.

105

106

107

108

Art Nouveau Style, 1896–1914

Sinuous curves dominate form and decoration. Common motifs are naturalistic and stylized tulips, lilies, poppies, and leaves. The Art Nouveau Style held limited appeal, and few examples survive.

An exposition at Paris in 1900 popularized this style internationally. It had originated in Paris, with encouragement by the art dealer Siegfried Bing. He featured it in his shop, known as the Maison de l'Art Nouveau, from 1896 until the shop closed in 1902. Designers created for Bing's clients costly handmade interpretations of their "Modern Art," which was inspired particularly by the curving line in Japanese art and French eighteenth-century Rococo art.

Sophisticated furniture reveals influence of the Art Nouveau Style, particularly in ornament, shortly before 1900 and until 1914. During this period, the style frequently influences curved lines in revival styles, and ornament occurs on mass-produced furniture as well as in the Arts and Crafts styles. There was a brief vogue among furniture manufacturers from 1900 to about 1903.

1. "Whiplash" curved lines
2. Gothic crockets
3. Form: Queen Anne Style revival
4. Relief-carved flower buds
5. Glass door
6. Mirrored back panel
7. Relief-carved poppies

105. Side chair, Charles Rohlfs, designer, Buffalo, New York, circa 1898; oak. The Art Museum, Princeton University, gift of Roland Rohlfs, Princeton, New Jersey.

106. Corner chair, probably New York City, 1900–1915; mahogany. The Art Institute of Chicago, gift of Dr. and Mrs. Edwin J. DeCosta, Chicago, Illinois.

107. Stand, United States, 1900–1915; mahogany. The Margaret Woodbury Strong Museum, Rochester, New York.

108. Cabinet, George C. Flint and Company, Chicago, Illinois, circa 1910; mahogany. The Metropolitan Museum of Art, Edgar J. Kauffmann, Jr., Charitable Foundation Fund, 1968, New York, New York.

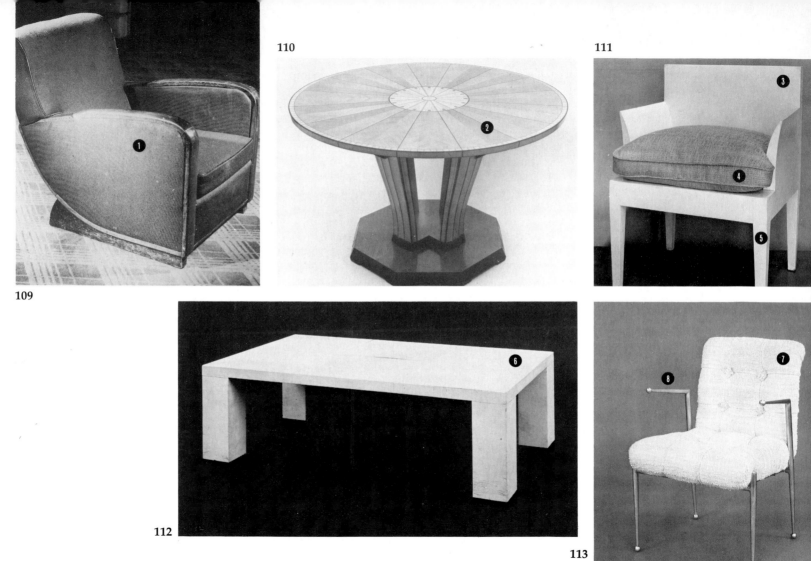

109

110

111

112

113

Art Deco Styles, 1925–1945

Controlled curves or crisp angles, monumental or delicate forms, and traditional wood or innovative steel are features of the greatly varying Art Deco movement in design. Common themes among the variations are simplicity of shape, emphasis on planes, and smooth surfaces.

Known to contemporaries as "Modern," the styles of the period are broadly identified today as "Art Deco." The term is derived from the Parisian event of 1925 that popularized the shift in taste and was titled "L'Exposition internationale des arts décorative et industriels modernes."

The immediate result of the exposition was a style of attenuated forms, lavish veneers, and boldly contrasting inlays in the tradition that Eero Saarinen commanded. Americans were equally open to other influences. Design gradually shifted in quality furniture of the 1930s to clarity of form as differently expressed as in the designs of Donald Deskey or Samuel Marx. Use of metal and experiments with construction reveal influences from the contemporary International Style abroad.

Fine craftsmanship and lavish materials are features of quality furniture. Surfaces vary from veneers and inlays of unusual woods to lacquer, parchment, and glass. The cocktail table is an innovation, chair backs are low and high, and upholstery varies from restrained to opulent.

1. Wool upholstery
2. Harewood veneer with ebony, box, holly inlays
3. White parchment surface
4. Wool cushion
5. Federal Style tapered leg
6. White leather surface
7. White wool upholstery
8. Steel

109. Armchair, Donald Deskey, designer, New York City, 1932; mahogany. Radio City Music Hall, New York, New York.

110. Dining table, Eliel Saarinen, designer for the Company of Master Craftsmen, Bloomfield Hills, Michigan, 1930; hare, ebony, box, and holly woods. The Cranbrook Academy of Art and Museum, Bloomfield Hills, Michigan.

111. Armchair, Hammond Kroll, designer, New York City, circa 1935; parchment over wood, with wool cushion, by Helen Kroll Kramer. The Smithsonian Institution, The Cooper-Hewitt Museum of Design, gift of Helen Kroll Kramer in memory of Dr. Milton Lurie, New York, New York.

112. Cocktail table, Samuel Marx, designer, Chicago, Illinois, 1944; white leather over wood. The Art Institute of Chicago, lent by Mr. and Mrs. Leigh B. Block, Chicago, Illinois.

113. Armchair, Donald Deskey, designer, New York City, circa 1935; steel, with wool upholstery, by Dorothy Liebes. The Art Institute of Chicago, gift of Mrs. Florene Schoenborn, Chicago, Illinois.

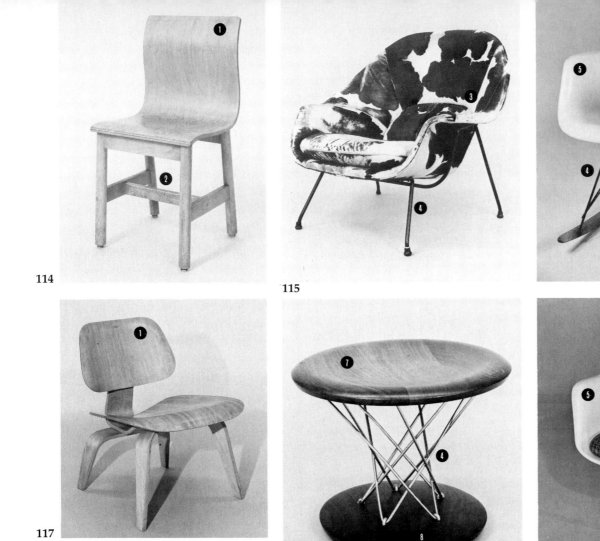

114

115

116

117

118

119

International Style, 1940–Present

Industrial materials and industrial production meet objectives of furniture independent of traditional styles. The concept originated in continental Europe after World War I.

The Bauhaus, a school founded in Germany at Weimar and later moved to Dessau and Berlin, became the center of the new movement in the 1920s through Walter Gropius, Ludwig Miës van der Rohe, and Marcel Breuer. These leaders of the Bauhaus and other immigrants in the 1930s established the approach in American design.

The Museum of Modern Art encouraged the movement in 1940 with a competition for domestic furnishings. Eero Saarinen and Charles Eames won first prizes for a chair design and standardized tables and case furniture. The revolutionary chair combined seat, back, and arms into one unit of laminated woods formed in a mold. The design potential was realized after World War II, when Saarinen and Eames became innovators in the movement for industrially produced furniture in plastic, plywood, and metal.

Breuer's intent and that of other Europeans in the 1920s and 1930s was furniture without "style." But furniture designed in the International Style clearly reveals different aesthetic preferences among designers, as well as the influence of other contemporary movements in the arts.

1. **Molded laminated woods**
2. **Medial and side stretchers**
3. **Cowhide over plastic**
4. **Steel**
5. **Molded plastic**
6. **Aluminum**
7. **Teak**
8. **Curved base**

114. Side chair, Eero Saarinen and Larry Perkins, designers for the Illinois WPA Craft Project, Chicago, Illinois, 1940; birch and laminated birch. The Art Institute of Chicago, gift of the Crow Island School, Chicago, Illinois.

115. Womb chair, Eero Saarinen, designer for Knoll International, East Greenville, Pennsylvania, 1948; steel, cowhide over plastic shell. The Art Institute of Chicago, gift of Mrs. Albert H. Newman, Chicago, Illinois.

116. Rocking chair for child, Charles Eames, designer for Herman Miller Furniture Company, Zeeland, Michigan, 1953; plastic, steel, birch. The Art Institute of Chicago, gift of Joseph H. Makler, Chicago, Illinois.

117. Side chair, Charles Eames, designer for Evans Products Company, Plymouth, Michigan, 1947–1949; laminated woods. The Art Institute of Chicago, gift of Mrs. Eugene A. Davidson, Chicago, Illinois.

118. Rocking stool, Isamu Noguchi, designer for Knoll International, East Greenville, Pennsylvania, 1950; teak, steel. The Art Institute of Chicago, gift of Joseph H. Makler, Chicago, Illinois.

119. Armchair, Eero Saarinen, designer for Knoll International, East Greenville, Pennsylvania, 1956; plastic, aluminum. The Art Institute of Chicago, gift of Knoll International, Chicago, Illinois.

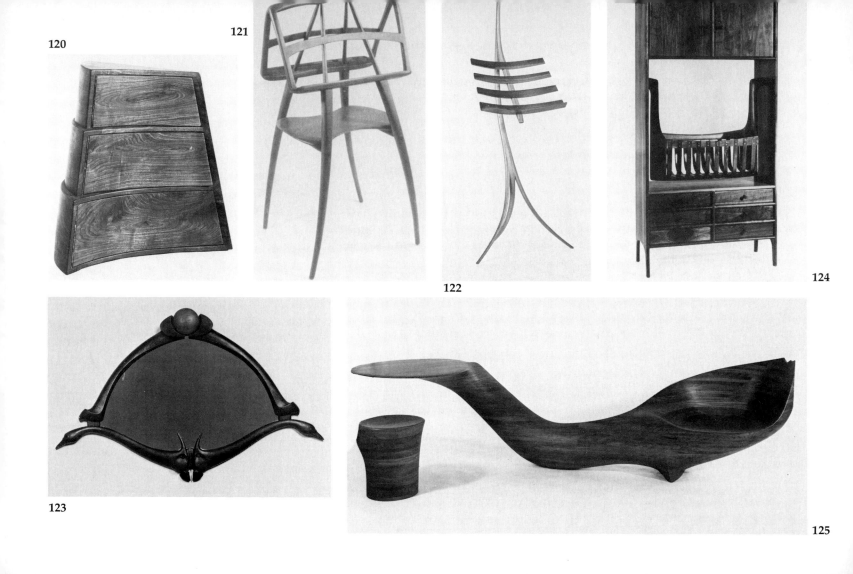

120

121

122

123

124

125

Craftsman and Contemporary Styles, 1945–Present

Execution varies from a craftsman's personally creating unique furniture to his supervising others in making his designs or variations of them. Iron or plastics are the materials of recent innovators, but the general concern is with the traditional material of wood.

The movement has evolved nationally since the late 1940s. It is a reaction to standardized industrial furniture, and it continues the philosophy of personal expression from the Arts and Crafts period. Wharton Esherick is a link to craftsmen and their ideals at the turn of the twentieth century through his example from the 1920s to the 1960s.

Personal styles reflect greatly varying intellectual and emotional responses to furniture as a practical, sculptural, or even a humorous element in daily life. Forms are rectilinear, abstract, and occasionally anthropomorphic and biomorphic.

Woods may be selected for uniformity of color and grain, chosen for irregularities, or laminated for the potential of form, strength, and decoration. Production is equally diverse. It may rely on hand craftsmanship or modern technology in any phase of preparing, forming, and finishing woods.

120. Chest-table, Wharton Esherick, Paoli, Pennsylvania, 1969; walnut. The American Craft Museum, gift of the Johnson Wax Company, New York, New York.

121. Double music rack, Wharton Esherick, Paoli, Pennsylvania, 1962; walnut, cherry. The Wharton Esherick Museum, Paoli, Pennsylvania.

122. Music rack, Wendell Castle, Scottsville, New York, 1964; oak, walnut, cherry. The American Craft Museum, New York, New York.

123. Looking glass, Daniel K. Jackson, Philadelphia, Pennsylvania, 1973; rosewood, Osage orange. The Philadelphia Museum of Art, gift of the Friends of the Philadelphia Museum of Art, Philadelphia, Pennsylvania.

124. Cradle-cabinet, Sam Maloof, Alta Loma, California, 1968; laminated walnut. The American Craft Museum, gift of the Johnson Wax Company, New York, New York.

125. Table-chair-stool, Wendell Castle, Scottsville, New York, 1968; afromosia. The American Craft Museum, gift of the Johnson Wax Company, New York, New York.

Dutch Style, 1624–1860

Seventeenth-century immigrants to Dutch claims in the mid-Atlantic region introduced furniture designs continuing in isolated areas in northern New Jersey, on Long Island, and in the Hudson River Valley long after the major settlement of New Amsterdam became the prominent English community of New York City. Diverse origins of the colonists in the Netherlands and their equally diverse sophistication are evident in the recorded furniture.

The practical *kas*, common in northern Europe during the seventeenth century for storing clothing, linens, and other personal articles, is a major form. It survives in many variations. They range from seventeenth-century versions in oak and eighteenth-century examples in walnut, maple, or tulip with painted decoration, to early nineteenth-century mahogany examples with inlays in the Federal Style.

Other furniture forms and their decoration reveal continental influences. Turnings are elaborate on chairs and tables. Curves are complex on cupboards or other forms, such as the multipurpose chair-table with a storage compartment beneath the chair seat and a back lowering to become a table top. Simple tables include stretchers between legs as well as central diagonal braces between top and base.

1. **Ovolo molding with raised panels**
2. **Fielded panels**
3. **Boss**
4. **Drawer**
5. **Ball foot**
6. **Finial**
7. **Blue-green paint**
8. **Flat arm rest**
9. **Turned support**
10. **Rush seat**
11. **Black, gray, white decoration**
12. **Back tilts for table**
13. **Seat lifts for storage**
14. **Medial stretcher**
15. **Trestle base**
16. **Distinctive cross-stretchers**
17. **Chamfered corner**

126. *Kas* (wardrobe), New York City area, 1650–1700; oak. The Art Institute of Chicago, Sanford Fund, Chicago, Illinois.

127. Armchair, Kings County, Queens County, or New York City, 1680–1700; oak painted blue-green. The Art Institute of Chicago, Sewell L. Avery Fund, Chicago, Illinois.

128. *Kas* (wardrobe), New York City area, 1700–1735; tulip with black, gray, white painted decoration. The Henry Francis du Pont Winterthur Museum, Winterthur, Delaware.

129. Chair-table, Hudson River Valley, 1690–1740; maple, oak. The Art Institute of Chicago, gift of Jamee J. Field and Marshall Field, in honor of Nancy J. Naeve and Milo M. Naeve, Chicago, Illinois.

130. Table, Hudson River Valley, 1725–1775; maple and tulip painted gray. Sleepy Hollow Restorations, Van Cortlandt Manor House, Tarrytown, New York.

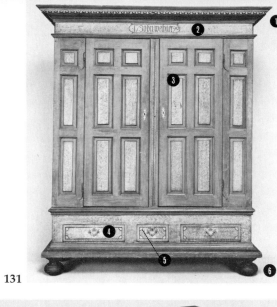

131

132

133

134

135

German Style, 1750–1870

Immigrants from the southern German states to southeastern Pennsylvania introduced a style flourishing by the late eighteenth century with emigration to Virginia, North Carolina, and Ohio. The Germans initially continued seventeenth- and eighteenth-century forms abroad for chairs, chests, tables, and other furniture. American variations of Germanic decorations soon were adapted to traditional chests, boxes, and wardrobes known as *shonks*, as well as to such English forms as chests of drawers, clocks, and desks with bookcases. The German Style flourished through the early nineteenth century. It lost vigor at mid-century, with the dissipation of German culture and access to mass-produced furniture.

Storage chests of tulip wood for men and women are the favored form. Elaborate versions are brightly painted in red, blue, white, and yellow, with tulips, hearts, birds, stars, and unicorns. Walnut inlaid with white sulpher designs of scrolls, pilasters, hearts, and shells are a distinctive and smaller group. Names and initials of owners and commemorative dates frequently document pride of possession.

1. Cornice with dentil variation
2. Owner name and date: "17 John Weidner 90"
3. Blue-green, coral, and white paint
4. Drawer
5. Painted version of Federal Style inlay
6. Ball foot
7. Hand grip
8. Legs extend through seat
9. Chamfered corners
10. Form adapts Philadelphia Chippendale Style
11. Blue-green and white paint
12. Bracket foot
13. Hinged top with battens
14. Sulphur inlay in walnut
15. Pilaster
16. Foliate scrolls
17. Blue, white, red, and black paint

131. *Shonk* (wardrobe), Oley area, Pennsylvania, 1790; tulip with blue, white, red painted decoration. The Art Institute of Chicago, Elizabeth R. Vaughan Fund, Chicago, Illinois.

132. Side chair, Zoar, Ohio, 1850–1875; pine, oak. Greenfield Village and Henry Ford Museum, Dearborn, Michigan.

133. Desk and bookcase, eastern Pennsylvania, 1780–1810; pine, painted blue-green and white. The Henry Francis du Pont Winterthur Museum, Winterthur, Delaware.

134. Chest, Ephrata area, Pennsylvania, 1783; walnut with sulphur inlay. The Smithsonian Institution, Washington, D.C.

135. Chest, Lebanon or Berks County, Pennsylvania, 1785–1800; tulip with blue, white, red, black painted decoration. The Virginia Museum of Fine Arts, the Williams Fund, Richmond, Virginia.

136

138

139

137

140

Spanish Style, 1600–1900

Furniture was rare in Spanish territories across the present southern United States. Surviving examples are mainly from New Mexico, where scarce tools, hinges, and locks were imported about 2,000 miles away from Mexico City.

Life in Santa Fe, founded in 1610, was simple. Beyond the capital, it was primitive. Until the nineteenth century, tables, chairs, benches, and beds were unknown except for those in churches or prosperous households. The earliest survivals are from the eighteenth century and continue traditions for simple furniture in seventeenth- and eighteenth-century Spain.

Chests are the common form. They rest on the floor, on stands, or on legs. The other traditional forms are *alcenas* (wall cupboards), *repisos* (shelves), *tarmitas* (stools), and *trasteros* (cupboards).

Decoration is simple. Chests, cupboards, and shelves include geometric designs or generalized motifs, such as flowers, shells, rosettes, scrolls, and occasionally animals. Motifs are carved in relief or painted in yellow, red, blue, black, and white. Grooves and chip carving are common.

Soft Ponderosa pine is the principal wood. The difficulty of preparing it, before the introduction of sawmills in 1846, resulted in reworking parts from worn or damaged furniture.

1. **Hinged top**
2. **Triangle motif**
3. **Fielded panel with relief carving**
4. **Channel molding**
5. **Relief-carved lions, rabbits, foliate scrolls**
6. **Exposed dovetail joint**
7. **Separate stand**
8. **Relief-carved panels of lions, rosettes, pomegranates**
9. **Batten**
10. **Exposed mortise-and-tenon joint**
11. **Hinged door with spindles**

136. Chest, northern New Mexico, 1830–1860, pine. The Millicent Rogers Museum, Taos, New Mexico.

137. Armchair, northern New Mexico, 1775–1800; pine. The Museum of New Mexico, Santa Fe, New Mexico.

138. Chest with stand, northern New Mexico, 1780–1820; pine. The Museum of New Mexico, Santa Fe, New Mexico.

139. Chest, northern New Mexico, 1780–1820; pine. The American Museum in Britain, Claverton Manor, Bath, England.

140. Food cupboard, northern New Mexico, 1800–1850; pine. The American Museum in Britain, Claverton Manor, Bath, England.

141

142

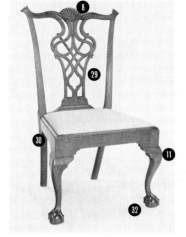

143

144

145

146

147

Vernacular Styles, 1670–1790

Furniture in many traditions includes six-board chests and trestle tables of the Medieval Style, joined and turned forms, modifications of sophisticated styles, or is new in concept. Spanish, Dutch, and German immigrants evolved other traditions, forming distinct styles.

Significant among designs original to America are late seventeenth-century dower chests, carved in low relief with tulips, hearts, and other motifs popular in the isolated Connecticut River Valley. They are known as "Hadley" chests—after the town of Hadley, Massachusetts—but craftsmen made them over several generations from Hartford, Connecticut, to Deerfield, Massachusetts.

Common chairs follow a European tradition of shaped slats and turned legs introduced in America during the seventeenth century. The many variations range from high backs in New England—influenced by chairs of the William and Mary Style—to walnut chairs delicate in appearance, yet sturdy in construction, from Pennsylvania.

Adaptations of sophisticated furniture may be contemporary with a style or may combine motifs from earlier styles. The furniture is decorated with simple carving and painted.

Woods usually are local. Birch and maple often are stained imitations of mahogany.

141. Chest ("Hadley" type), Connecticut River Valley, 1670–1720; oak, white pine. The Art Institute of Chicago, gift of the Robert R. McCormick Charitable Trust, Chicago, Illinois.

142. Chest-on-chest, on frame, possibly by Samuel Dunlap, New Hampshire, 1780–1820; maple. The Currier Gallery of Art, Manchester, New Hampshire.

143. Table, Connecticut or western Massachusetts, 1710–1740; cherry and maple, painted red. Historic Deerfield, Inc., Deerfield, Mass.

144. Side chair, possibly Rhode Island, 1690–1730; maple painted blue-green. The Art Institute of Chicago, Wirt D. Walker Fund, Chicago.

145. Highchair for child, Pennsylvania, 1740–1775; walnut. The Art Institute of Chicago, gift of the Barker Welfare Foundation, Chicago, Illinois.

146. Side chair, William Savery, Philadelphia, Pennsylvania, 1746–1760; maple. The Art Institute of Chicago, gift of the Antiquarian Society, Chicago, Illinois.

147. Side chair, South Windsor area, Connecticut, 1771–1807; mahogany. The Art Institute of Chicago, gift of the Antiquarian Society, Chicago, Illinois.

1. Hinged top with battens
2. Relief-carved tulips, leaves, hearts
3. Side rail
4. Muntin
5. Stile
6. Knob handle
7. Cornice
8. Scallop shell
9. Carved ogee molding
10. S scroll
11. Cabriole leg
12. Square pad foot
13. Hinged leaf
14. "Butterfly" leaf support
15. Splay leg
16. Double baluster turning
17. Stretcher base
18. Worn ball foot
19. Finial
20. Turned posts
21. Splint seat
22. Concave arm for tying child
23. Footrest
24. Crest rail with yoke
25. Concave, urn-shaped splat
26. Side, medial, and back stretchers
27. Leaf-carving at knee
28. Triphid foot with raised panels
29. Chinese fret
30. Side rail
31. Front rail
32. Claw-and-ball foot

148

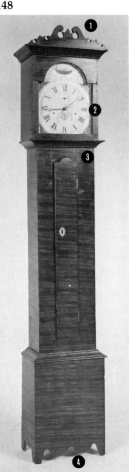

149

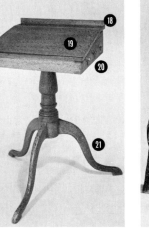

150

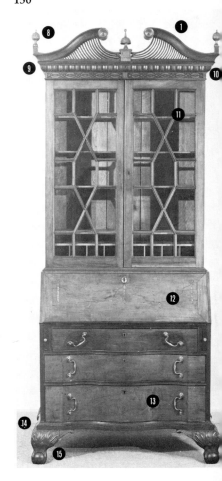

151

152

153

Vernacular Styles, 1791–1914

The great variety of the eighteenth century gradually decreases, with developing mass production. By the 1870s, factories replace the efforts of most local craftsmen.

The early nineteenth century includes variations of many styles. Chests and tables still occur in the Medieval Style. Simple beds follow the seventeenth- and eighteenth-century form. Descendants of Spanish, Dutch, and German immigrants continue their distinctive styles. Adaptations of the Queen Anne, Chippendale, and Federal styles continue in isolated areas. Shakers produce simple designs into the early nineteenth century in their distinctive style.

Designs are carved with less frequency, as training and skills decline. Decoration increasingly is achieved by red, blue, yellow, or white paint, by simulating mahogany and maple grains, or by working simple designs into wet paint. By the 1830s, stencil decoration is common. Chairs by the Hitchcock factory and others gradually complement those in the Windsor Style, as furniture-production becomes an industry.

Rustic furniture of tree limbs with the bark intact evolves in the mid-nineteenth century as one of the styles for garden furniture. It continues into the early twentieth century, as furniture in rural areas, mountain lodges, or informal rooms.

1. Broken-arch pediment
2. Face (dial and spandrels)
3. Red and brown paint
4. Scalloped apron in Queen Anne Style
5. Low-post bedstead (wooden frame)
6. Headboard
7. Rope
8. Finial
9. Ovolo molding with egg-and-dart motif
10. Blind Chinese fret
11. Mullions
12. Inlaid festoon in Federal Style
13. Serpentine curve
14. Two-relief carved scallop shells of Queen Anne Style
15. Claw-and-ball foot of Chippendale Style
16. Gilt stencil decoration
17. Rush seat
18. Yellow and brown paint
19. Writing surface
20. Drawers
21. Cabriole leg of Queen Anne Style
22. Hickory with bark intact
23. Shaped-oak back and seat

148. Clock, Silas Hoadley, Plymouth, Connecticut, 1813–circa 1823; white pine painted red and brown. The Art Institute of Chicago, gift of Mr. Marshall Field, Mr. Charles C. Haffner III, Mrs. Burton W. Hales, Mrs. C. Phillip Miller, Mrs. Clive Runnells, and Mrs. Frank L. Sulzburger, Chicago, Illinois.

149. Bedstead, Massachusetts, 1800–1850; ash. The Henry Francis du Pont Winterthur Museum, gift of Joseph Downs, Winterthur, Delaware.

150. Desk and bookcase, John Shearer, Martinsburg, West Virginia, 1801; cherry, walnut, oak, mulberry. The Museum of Early Southern Decorative Arts, Winston-Salem, North Carolina.

151. Side chair, probably New York City, 1815–1830; red and brown paint with gilt stencil decoration. The Art Institute of Chicago, gift of Mr. and Mrs. Edwin N. Asmann, Chicago, Illinois.

152. Writing stand, New England, 1815–1840; maple and white pine painted yellow and brown. The Art Institute of Chicago, Bessie Bennett Fund, Chicago, Illinois.

153. Rocking chair, southern Ohio, 1890–1910; hickory frame, oak seat, back, and rockers. The Art Institute of Chicago, gift of Mr. and Mrs. Robert A. Kubicek, Chicago, Illinois.

154

155

156

157

158

Shaker Style, 1800–1914

Efficient design and effective craftsmanship support principles of the United Society of Believers in Christ's Second Appearing. In 1774, nine members of the celibate sect that would become known as "Shakers," because of movements during ritual dances used in their worship, came to America from England. Conversions reached a peak in the 1840s, with about 6,000 members in communal centers from New England and the South to the Midwest.

Shaker furniture design generally follows early-nineteenth-century simple traditions familiar to the membership. Shakers made most of their furniture for dormitories and workshops, but in Mount Lebanon, New York, they made chairs and stools for public sale in the late nineteenth and early twentieth centuries. Later furniture also includes simplified motifs from sophisticated styles.

Shaker practicality encouraged such features as low-backed chairs that could be stored under dining tables, wheels on beds, and storage drawers built into walls. Early furniture is painted. By the mid-nineteenth century, stains, clear varnish, and shellac enhance grain and color of woods, which are functional as well as decorative. Easily shaped hickory or oak serves as chair slats, durable maple is used for drawer knobs, and dense cherry for table tops. Other woods include butternut, chestnut, pear, and walnut, as well as easily worked pine. Slight differences between various Shaker workshops are particularly evident in chairs through finial design, number and design of slats, and the varied use of straw, reed, or tape for seats.

1. **Low-post bedstead (wooden frame)**
2. **Acorn-shaped finial**
3. **Headboard**
4. **Footboard**
5. **Side rail**
6. **Maple wheel**
7. **Cabriole leg, of Queen Anne Style**
8. **Slat back**
9. **Splint seat**
10. **Drawer with knob handle**
11. **Slide for work surface**
12. **Bracket foot of Queen Anne Style**
13. **Rush seat**

154. Bed, Mount (New) Lebanon, New York, Shaker Community, 1800–1830; chestnut posts, pine footboard, headboard, and rails, maple wheels. The Henry Francis du Pont Winterthur Museum, gift of Miss Helen Brown, Miss Margaret Brown, and Miss Pauline Brown, Winterthur, Delaware.

155. Stand, attributed to Enfield, Connecticut, Shaker Community, 1790–1830; cherry. The Henry Francis du Pont Winterthur Museum, Winterthur, Delaware.

156. Rocking chair, attributed to Mount (New) Lebanon, New York, Shaker Community, 1800–1830; birch, maple. The Henry Francis du Pont Winterthur Museum, Winterthur, Delaware; gift of the Halcyon Foundation, the American Museum in Britain.

157. Desk, unidentified Shaker community, United States, 1800–1850; ash, pine. Henry Francis du Pont Winterthur Museum, Winterthur, Delaware.

158. Dining chair, Mount (New) Lebanon, New York, Shaker Community, 1873–circa 1883; maple. The Art Institute of Chicago, gift of Mrs. Len H. Small, Chicago, Illinois.

159

160

161

162

163

164

Windsor Style, 1750–Present

Windsor Style furniture parts interlock for strength through tension. Side chairs complement armchairs by the 1770s, and settees are popular by the 1790s, with occasional stools and tables.

Woods selected for function include hard oak for arms or crests, dense maple for legs, supple hickory and birch for spindles or crests, and soft ash, tulip, or pine for shaped seats. By the mid-nineteenth century, color and grain are decorative features, instead of red, yellow, blue-green, or white paint. Rare eighteenth-century Windsors with cabriole legs and pad feet are made of walnut, a wood recurring in the mid-twentieth century.

Craftsmen specialize in Windsors until the early 1800s, by making or buying interchangeable parts. After nineteenth-century factory production, independent craftsmen return in the mid-twentieth century.

The English origin of Windsor furniture is uncertain, although Windsors are identified with the English village of Windsor until the early nineteenth century. Rural English craftsmen were developing the style by the early 1700s, and it reached Philadelphia at mid-century. By the Revolution, variations occur throughout the colonies for elegant, as well as plain, houses and for gardens. Decorative turnings are baluster shapes in the eighteenth century, bamboo shapes after the Revolution, concentric rings in the mid-nineteenth century; in the mid-twentieth century, they disappear.

1. **Crest rail with volutes**
2. **Doric column**
3. **Baluster turning**
4. **Brace**
5. **Blue-green paint over surface**
6. **Medial and side stretchers**
7. **Cabriole leg and pad foot of Queen Anne Style**
8. **Bamboo-shaped turnings**
9. **Brown and red paint**
10. **Gilt stencil decoration**
11. **Varnish finish**
12. **Trestle base**

159. Windsor armchair, Philadelphia, Pennsylvania, 1750–1775; tulip seat, maple legs, hickory spindles, oak arms, painted blue-green. The Art Institute of Chicago, gift of Elizabeth R. Vaughan, Chicago, Illinois.

160. Windsor armchair, Philadelphia, Pennsylvania, 1750–1775; walnut. The Art Institute of Chicago, gift of Mrs. Christopher Brown, Mr. Marshall Field, Mrs. Harold T. Martin, Mrs. H. Alex Vance, and Mary Waller Langhorne Fund, Chicago, Illinois.

161. Windsor settee, probably Pennsylvania, 1785–1800; oak spindles, crest rail, arms; tulip seat; maple legs, stretchers, and rear stiles; painted brown over red and blue-green. The Yale University Art Gallery, Mabel Brady Garvan Collection, New Haven, Connecticut.

162. Windsor rocking chair, New England, 1830–1850; hickory or oak spindles, pine seat, maple legs and arms, painted brown and red with gilt stencil decoration. Greenfield Village and Henry Ford Museum, Dearborn, Michigan.

163. Windsor side chair for child, probably New England, 1880–1890; oak rail, ash seat, birch spindles. Mark Twain Memorial, Hartford, Connecticut.

164. Windsor side chair, George Nakashima, New Hope, Pennsylvania, 1962; walnut with hickory spindles. Courtesy George Nakashima, New Hope, Pennsylvania.

165

166

167

168

169 170

171

Garden Furniture Styles, 1800–1914

Windsors graced gardens and houses until the early nineteenth century. Chairs made in factories replaced Windsors indoors by mid-century as a new and substantial furniture became available outdoors.

Iron production had greatly advanced from the late eighteenth to the mid-nineteenth centuries in England. Costs were reduced and casting improved for delicacy in details and greater size in parts. Legs, backs, and seats could be made as standard parts, shipped, and assembled with screws. Occasional furniture in the Gothic Style led to widespread production of tables, chairs, and settees in the Rococo Revival Style. General popularity with this style led to designs in all of the later styles. They were disseminated from England and within America, as the product of one manufacturer easily served as the pattern for another's mold.

Wire production encouraged a new kind of furniture by the 1870s. Interlaced designs provided both strength and decoration in chairs, stands, and settees.

Native willow and imported rattan offered materials for a wide range of simple and elaborate forms after the War Between the States. The furniture also served informally in houses by the late nineteenth and early twentieth centuries.

Rustic furniture of gnarled tree limbs with the bark intact gained popularity at mid-century with the Naturalistic Style. Most of the survivals are from the late nineteenth century, when the approach became common, not only in gardens, but also in mountain lodges and in vernacular furniture throughout the United States.

1. **Gothic Revival Style**
2. **Rococo Revival Style**
3. **Renaissance Revival Style**
4. **Classical influence**
5. **Lancet arch of Gothic Revival Style**
6. **Japanese design influence**

165. Settee, probably New York, circa 1836; cast-iron. Sleepy Hollow Restorations, Sunnyside, Tarrytown, New York.

166. Side chair, Robert Wood and Company, Philadelphia, Pennsylvania, 1850–1860; cast-iron. Greenfield Village and Henry Ford Museum, Dearborn, Michigan.

167. Table, United States, 1850–1870; cast-iron. The Metropolitan Museum of Art, Anonymous Gift Fund, 1968, New York, New York.

168. Urn, Van Dorn Iron Works, Cleveland, Ohio, 1850–1885; cast-iron. The Metropolitan Museum of Art, Edgar J. Kauffmann, Jr., Charitable Foundation Fund, 1969, New York, New York.

169. Settee, Colt Willow Ware Works, Hartford, Connecticut, circa 1855–1873; willow. The Wadsworth Atheneum, Colt Collection, Hartford, Connecticut.

170. Side chair, United States, 1875–1880; wire. Greenfield Village and Henry Ford Museum, Dearborn, Michigan.

171. Settee, the Kramer Brothers, Dayton, Ohio, 1905–1925; cast-iron. The Art Institute of Chicago, gift of Mrs. Burton W. Hales, through the Antiquarian Society, Chicago, Illinois.

Further Reading

Publications traditionally have followed the interests of private and institutional collectors by emphasizing furniture of New England and furniture made through the early nineteenth century. Concern, especially developing over the last two decades, for furniture in every region of the United States and through the period immediately after World War II has encouraged a broader scope of documentation. That concern is revealed in the publications selected for the even focus of this guide on the major styles in American furniture.

Periodicals

The American Art Journal, 1969—
Antiques, 1922—
Antiques World, 1978—
Arts and Antiques, 1978—
Furniture History, 1965—
The Journal of Early Southern Decorative Arts, 1975—
Nineteenth Century, 1975—
Winterthur Portfolio, 1964—

Books and Articles

Background Sources: Architecture and Design

Agius, Pauline. *British Furniture: 1880–1915*. Woodbridge, Suffolk, England: Baron Publishing for the Antique Collectors' Club, 1978. Illustrated survey of mass-produced, as well as custom-designed, furniture.

Blumenson, John J.-G. *Identifying American Architecture: A Pictorial Guide to Styles and Terms, 1600–1945*. Nashville: The American Association for State and Local History, 1977. Introduction to architectural styles, comparable to this guide for furniture, with pictorial glossary of classical and other architectural motifs often adapted to furniture.

Ellsworth, Robert Hatfield. *Chinese Furniture: Hardwood Examples of the Ming and Early Ch'ing Dynasties.* New York: Random House, 1971. Authoritative presentation of stylistic and technical information.

Hayward, Helena, ed. *World Furniture*. New York and Toronto: McGraw-Hill Book Co., 1965. Written by specialists, the book is the most authoritative survey published.

Macquoid, Percy, and Ralph Edwards. *The Dictionary of English Furniture from the Middle Ages to the Late Georgian Period*. 3 vols. Charles Scribner's Sons: New York, 1924. Illustrated survey of sophisticated and vernacular furniture with reliable definitions of terms.

Richter, Gisela Marie Augusta. *The Furniture of the Greeks, Etruscans and Romans*. London: Phaidon, 1966. Authoritative presentation with excellent bibliography.

General Sources: American Furniture

Ames, Kenneth L. "What is neo-grec?" and "Sitting in [Neo-Grec] Style." *Nineteenth Century* 2, nos. 2, 3–4 (Summer, Autumn 1976): 13–21 and 51–58.

Bishop, Robert. *Centuries and Styles of the American Chair, 1640–1970*. New York: E. P. Dutton & Co., 1972.

Butler, Joseph T. *American Antiques, 1800–1900: A Collector's History and Guide*. New York: The Odyssey Press, 1965.

Clark, Robert Judson, et al. *The Arts and Crafts Movement in America*. Princeton: Princeton University Press, 1972.

Comstock, Helen. *American Furniture: Seventeenth, Eighteenth, and Nineteenth Century Styles*. New York: The Viking Press, 1962.

Cooper, Wendy A. *In Praise of America: American Decorative Arts, 1650–1830: Fifty Years of Discovery Since the 1929 Girl Scouts Loan Exhibition*. New York: Alfred A. Knopf, 1980.

Downs, Joseph. *American Furniture: Queen Anne and Chippendale Periods in the Henry Francis du Pont Winterthur Museum*. New York: The Macmillan Co., 1952.

Gowans, Alan. *Images of American Living: Four Centuries of Architecture and Furniture as Cultural Expression*. Philadelphia and New York: J. B. Lippincott Co., 1964.

Hillier, Bevis. "Furniture." In *Art Deco*, pp. 52–63. Minneapolis: The Minneapolis Institute of Arts, 1971.

Howe, Katherine S., and David B. Warren, with introduction by Jane B. Davies. *The Gothic-Revival Style in America, 1830–1870*. Houston: The Museum of Fine Arts, Houston, 1976.

Hummel, Charles F. *A Winterthur Guide to American Chippendale Furniture: Middle Atlantic and Southern Colonies*. New York: Crown Publishers, Inc., for Rutledge Books, 1976.

Israel Sack, Inc. *Opportunities in American Antiques*. New York: Israel Sack, Inc., 1957—Occasional brochures with illustrations and comments about furniture for sale during the seventeenth, eighteenth, and early nineteenth centuries. Brochures are collected and republished in book form as *American Antiques from Israel Sack Collection*. Washington, D.C.: Highland House Publishers, Inc., 1969 (vol. 1)—

Johnson, Marilynn; Marvin D. Schwartz; Suzanne Boorsch; and Berry B. Tracy. *19th-Century America: Furniture and Other Decorative Arts: An Exhibition in Celebration of the Hundredth Anniversary of the Metropolitan Museum of Art, April 6 through September 7, 1970*. New York: The Metropolitan Museum of Art, 1970. Furniture text by Ms. Johnson. Other decorative arts by Mr. Schwartz and Ms. Boorsch. Introduction by Berry B. Tracy.

Kane, Patricia E. *300 Years of American Seating Furniture: Chairs and Beds from the Mabel Brady Garvan and Other Collections at Yale University*. Boston: New York Graphic Society, 1976.

Kassay, John. *The Book of Shaker Furniture*. Amherst: The University of Massachusetts Press, 1980.

Madigan, Mary Jean Smith. *Eastlake-Influenced American Furniture, 1870–1890*. Yonkers: The Hudson-River Museum, 1973.

Meader, Robert F. *Illustrated Guide to Shaker Furniture*. New York: Dover Publications, Inc., 1972.

Montgomery, Charles F. *American Furniture: The Federal Period in the Henry Francis du Pont Winterthur Museum*. New York: The Viking Press, 1966.

Morse, John D., ed. *Country Cabinetwork and Simple City Furniture*. Charlottesville: The University Press of Virginia for the Henry Francis du Pont Winterthur

Museum, 1970. Articles by seven specialists about vernacular furniture to 1840.

Naeve, Milo M. *The Classical Presence in American Art.* Chicago: The Art Institute of Chicago, 1978. Illustrated essay about Greek and Roman influences on American art, including furniture, from the seventeenth to the twentieth centuries.

Page, Marion. *Furniture Designed by Architects.* New York: Whitney Library of Design, 1980. Emphasis on American architects of the nineteenth and twentieth centuries.

Pilgrim, Dianne H. "Decorative Art: The Domestic Environment." In *The American Renaissance: 1876–1917,* pp. 110–151. Brooklyn: The Brooklyn Museum, 1979.

Quimby, Ian M. G., ed. *Arts of the Anglo-American Community in the Seventeenth Century.* Charlottesville: The University Press of Virginia for the Henry Francis du Pont Winterthur Museum, 1975. See especially Patricia E. Kane, "The Seventeenth-Century Furniture of the Connecticut Valley: The Hadley Chest Reappraised," pp. 79–122; Robert F. Trent, "The Joiners and Joinery of Middlesex County, Massachusetts, 1630–1730," pp. 123–148; and other articles presenting the background of American furniture in English and Dutch furniture.

Randall, Richard H. *American Furniture in the Museum of Fine Arts, Boston.* Boston: The Museum of Fine Arts, 1965.

Renwick Gallery of the National Collection of Fine Arts, Smithsonian Institution, Washington, D.C., and the Minnesota Museum of Art. *Woodenworks: George Nakashima, Sam Maloof, Wharton Esherick, Arthur Espenet Carpenter, and Wendell Castle.* St. Paul: The Minnesota Museum of Art, 1972.

Sack, Albert. *Fine Points of Furniture: Early American.* New York: Crown Publishers, Inc., 1950. Unique guide to quality in furniture through the early nineteenth century.

Smith, Paul J., et al. *New Handmade Furniture.* New York: American Craft Museum, 1979.

Teller, Betty. "American Furniture in the Art Nouveau Style." In *Art & Antiques* 3, no. 3 (May–June 1980): 96–101.

Warren, David B. *Bayou Bend: American Furniture, Paintings and Silver from the Bayou Bend Collection.* Houston: The Museum of Fine Arts, 1975.

Regional Sources: Mid-Atlantic

Dorman, Charles G. *Delaware Cabinetmakers and Allied Artisans, 1655–1855.* Wilmington: The Historical Society of Delaware, 1960.

Fabian, Monroe H. *The Pennsylvania-German Decorated Chest.* New York: Universe Books, 1978.

Failey, Dean F. *Long Island Is My Nation: The Decorative Arts and Craftsmen, 1640–1830.* Setauket: Society for the Preservation of Long Island Antiquities, 1977.

Horner, William Macpherson, Jr. *Blue Book, Philadelphia Furniture: William Penn to George Washington with Special Reference to the Philadelphia Chippendale School.* Philadelphia: Privately printed, 1935. 2nd printing with index and revised captions, Washington, D.C.: Highland House Publishers, Inc., 1977.

Hummel, Charles F. *With Hammer in Hand: The Dominy Craftsmen of East Hampton, New York.* University Press of Virginia for the Winterthur Museum, 1968. Furniture, tools, materials, and craft procedures of the Dominy family in the eighteenth and early nineteenth centuries offer an insight into practices elsewhere.

Kindig, Joseph K., III. *The Philadelphia Chair, 1685–1785.* York, Pa.: The Historical Society of York County, Pennsylvania, 1978.

Miller, V. Isabelle. *Furniture by New York Cabinetmakers: 1650 to 1860.* New York: The Museum of the City of New York, 1956.

Rice, Norman S. *New York Furniture before 1840 in the Collection of the Albany Institute of History and Art.* Albany: The Albany Institute, 1962.

Schiffer, Margaret Berwind. *Furniture and Its Makers of Chester County, Pennsylvania.* Philadelphia: University of Pennsylvania Press, 1966.

Schwartz, Marvin D., Edward Stanek, and Douglas True. *The Furniture of John Henry Belter and the Rococo Revival.* New York: E. P. Dutton, 1981.

Sewell, Darrel, et al. *Philadelphia: Three Centuries of American Art.* Philadelphia: The Philadelphia Museum of Art, 1976.

White, Margaret E. *Early Furniture Made in New Jersey, 1690–1870.* Newark: The Newark Museum Association, 1958.

Regional Sources: Midwest

Sikes, Jane E. *The Furniture Makers of Cincinnati, 1790 to 1849.* Cincinnati: Privately printed, 1976.

Spencer, Brian A., ed. *The Prairie School Tradition.* New York: Watson-Guptil Publications, 1979.

Regional Sources: New England

Fales, Dean A., Jr., et al. *Samuel McIntire: A Bicentennial Symposium, 1757–1957.* Salem: The Essex Institute, 1957.

Fales, Dean A., Jr. *The Furniture of Historic Deerfield.* New York: E. P. Dutton and Co., 1976.

Garvin, Donna-Belle; James L. Garvin; and John F. Page. *Plain and Elegant, Rich and Common: Documented New Hampshire Furniture, 1750–1850.* Concord: New Hampshire Historical Society, 1979.

Greenlaw, Barry A. *New England Furniture at Williamsburg.* Williamsburg: The Colonial Williamsburg Foundation, 1974.

Kane, Patricia E. *Furniture of the New Haven Colony: The Seventeenth-Century Style.* New Haven: The New Haven Colony Historical Society, 1973.

Kenney, John Tarrant. *The Hitchcock Chair.* New York: C. N. Potter, 1971.

Luther, Clair Franklin. *The Hadley Chest.* Hartford: Privately printed, 1935. For recent research, see above, Patricia E. Kane in Quimby, *Art of the Anglo-American Community . . .* and Richard Lawrence Green, "Fertility Symbols on the Hadley Chests," *Antiques* 112 (August 1977): 250–257.

Maynard, Henry P., and John T. Kirk. *Connecticut Furniture: Seventeenth and Eighteenth Centuries.* Hartford: The Wadsworth Atheneum, 1967.

Ott, Joseph K., et al. *The John Brown House Loan Exhibition of Rhode Island Furniture.* Providence: The Rhode Island Historical Society, 1965.

Parsons, Charles S. *The Dunlaps and Their Furniture.* Manchester, New Hampshire: The Currier Gallery of Art, 1970.

St. George, Robert Blair. *The Wrought Covenant: Source Material for the Study of Craftsmen and Community in Southeastern New England, 1620–1700.* Brockton, Mass.: Brockton Art Center and Fuller Memorial, 1979.

Trent, Robert Francis. "The Endicott Chairs." *Essex Institute Historical Collections* 114, no. 2 (April 1978): 103–119. Documentation of the armchair shown as Fig. 15 in this guide, with information about production of other chairs in Boston from 1660 to 1695.

Whitehill, Walter Muir, ed., assisted by Brock W. Jobe. *Boston Furniture of the Eighteenth Century.* Boston: The Colonial Society of Massachusetts, 1974. Written by nine specialists, the book presents research resulting from a conference and exhibition organized by Jonathan Fairbanks on the organization of the furniture industry, forms, decoration, and woods. A checklist of craftsmen and a bibliography on individual craftsmen are included.

Regional Sources: South

Baltimore Museum of Art. *Baltimore Furniture: The Work of Baltimore and Annapolis Cabinetmakers from 1760 to 1810.* Baltimore: The Baltimore Museum of Art, 1947.

Burton, E. Milby. *Charleston Furniture, 1700–1825.* Charleston: The Charleston Museum, 1955.

Coons, Betty C. *Antique By-Lines (Southern Vintage).* Richmond: The Guild of the Valentine Museum, 1979.

Elder, William Voss, III. *Baltimore Painted Furniture, 1800–1840.* Baltimore: The Baltimore Museum of Art, 1972.

Elder, William Voss, III. *Maryland Queen Anne and Chippendale Furniture of the Eighteenth Century.* Baltimore: October House, Inc., for the Baltimore Museum of Art, 1968.

Green, Henry D. *Furniture of the Georgia Piedmont Before 1830.* Atlanta: The High Museum of Art, 1976.

Page, Addison Franklin. *Kentucky Furniture.* Louisville: J. B. Speed Art Museum, 1974.

Poesch, Jessie J. *Early Furniture of Louisiana, 1750–1830.* New Orleans: Louisiana State Museum, 1972.

Stitt, Susan. *Museum of Early Southern Decorative Arts.* Winston-Salem: Old Salem, Inc., 1972.

Theus, Mrs. Charlton M. *Savannah Furniture, 1735–1825.* Savannah: Privately printed, 1967.

Regional Sources: Southwest

Boyd, E. "Woodworking." *Popular Arts of Spanish New Mexico*, pp. 246–265. Santa Fe: Museum of New Mexico Press, 1974.

Vedder, Alan C. *Furniture of Spanish New Mexico*. Santa Fe: The Sunstone Press, 1977.

Regional Sources: West

Anderson, Timothy J., et al. *California Design, 1910*. Los Angeles: California Design Center, 1974.

Current, William R., and Karen Current. *Greene and Greene: Architects in the Residential Style*. Fort Worth: Amon Carter Museum of Western Art, 1974.

Morningstar, Connie. *Early Utah Furniture*. Logan: The Utah State University Press, 1976.

Index

References are to illustrations. Forms, craftsmen, designers, and manufacturers are included. Motifs are identified by major interpretations in differing periods. Styles are easily located through the table of contents, and the reader is advised to consult commentaries pertinent to an inquiry.

Acanthus leaf, 33, 43, 45, 64, 77
Aluminum, 119
Anthemion, 45, 81
Apron (skirt), 11, 29, 67
Arch: Lancet, 54, 170; Gothic, 45, 165; Ogee, 53; Roman, 10; Trefoil, 52
Astragal (bead) molding, 8; double, 22

Ball-and-ring turning, 19
Ball foot, 12, 80, 90, 92, 97, 113, 126, 131
Ball turning, 16, 61
Baluster turning, 17, 58, 80, 159; double baluster, 18, 143
Bamboo turning, 98, 161
Basket-of-flowers motif, 39, 70, 78
Batten, 135, 139
Bead (astragal) molding, 8; double, 22
Bedstead: lowpost, 149, 154; highpost, 23; other, 43, 83, 98
Belter, John Henry, 68, 70
Blind fret, 150
Bombé case form, 34
Bookcase, 90, 93
Boss, 9, 85, 126
Box, 6
Bracket, 11, 33, 90, 93
Bracket foot: straight, 94, 131, 135, 157; ogee, 32, 133
Broken-arch pediment, 25, 29, 31, 133, 148, 150
Brooks, Thomas, 53
Butterfly table, 143
Byrne, Richard, 52

C scroll, 15, 30, 63, 68
Cabinet, 73, 75, 85, 94, 108, 124
Cabriole leg, 24, 47, 64, 70, 77, 142, 106, 152, 155, 160, 166
Caning, 41
Canted corner, 51
Card table, 39, 44, 48, 72
Cartouche, 63
Castle, Wendell, 122, 125
Castor, 46, 58
Cavetta molding, 22
Ceramic decoration, 73, 75, 93
Chair-Table, 129
Chamber table, 14
Chamfer, 3, 90, 130, 131
Channel molding, 11
Chest, 4, 10, 134, 135, 136, 138, 139, 141
Chest of drawers, 12, 34, 40, 55, 59, 103, 120, 124
Chest-on-chest, 142
Child, furniture for: high chair, 5, 145; rocker, 116; stool, 118; Windsor, 163
Chip carving, 6
Clark, John, 78
Claw-and-ball foot, 33, 62, 87, 150
Clock, 31, 96
Cleat, 4
Cloven-hoof foot, 84
Cluster column, 55, 78, 89
Cocktail table, 112
Colt Willow Ware Works, 169
Column: Cluster, 78, 89, 155; Doric, 8, 31, 159; Ionic, 74, 94; Octagonal, 56; Tuscan, 17
Company of Master Craftsmen, 110
Compass decoration, 4
Compass seat shape, 24
Concentric circle motif, 51
Console motif, 63, 80
Corner chair, 106
Cornice, 45, 142

Cornucopia, 41, 46
Crest (chair), 17
Crest rail, 33
Crocket, 52, 105
Croome, George, 85
Cupboard, food, 140
Curule chair, 82
Cyma molding, 18
Cyma reversa molding, 13

Davis, Alexander Jackson, 52
Daybed (méridienne), 50
Dennis, Thomas, 7
Dentil, 131
Desk, 21, 32, 99, 101, 152, 157
Desk and bookcase, 20, 133, 150
Deskey, Donald, 109, 113
Dessoir, Julius, 80
Dial (clock), 31, 148
Diaper design, 67
Dining table, 2, 18, 130; extension, 36, 110
Disc, on pad foot, 28
Dolphin motif, 43
Doric column, 8, 31, 159
Double baluster turning, 18
Dovetail joint, 138
Dressing table, 28
Drop, 14

Eagle motif, 42
Eames, Charles, 116, 117
Easy chair, 19
Egg-and-dart motif, 6, 73, 150
Ellis, Harvey, 104
Elmslie, George Grant, 96, 102
Esherick, Wharton, 120, 121
Étagère, 57, 63, 64
Evans Products Company, 117

Face (clock), 31, 148
Festoon, 25, 35, 150
Fielded panel, 126, 136
Finial: chair, 5, 7, 17, 60, 127, 144, 156, 158; clock, 31, 96; desk and bookcase, 133, 150
Flint, George C., and Company, 108
Flitch (veneer), 22
Floral motif, 10, 39, 59, 60, 63, 65, 67, 69, 70, 72, 75, 77, 78, 91, 94, 95, 97, 103, 106, 108, 135, 138, 139, 141, 171
Fluting, 29, 36
Foliate scroll, 7
Footboard (bed), 23
Fret, Chinese, 94, 147, 150

Gadrooning, 30, 45
Gaming table, 30
Gate-leg table, 18
Gothic arch, 45
Grapes-and-leaves motif, 69
Grecian couch, 46
Greek key motif, 85
Greene, Charles, 103
Grotesque, 3, 77

Hadley chest, 141
Headboard (bed), 23, 149
Herman Miller Furniture Company, 116
Herringbone banding, 21
Herter Brothers, 95
High chair, 5, 145
High chest of drawers, 22, 25, 29
Hoadley, Silas, 148
Homes, William and Company, 90
Hood (pediment), 20
Husk, 36

Inlay, 21, 36, 37, 38, 95, 96, 104, 110
Ionic column, 74, 94

Jackson, Daniel K., **123**
Japanning, 25
Jelliff, John, 79
Johnson, Thomas, 25

Kas (wardrobe), 126, 128
Klismos chair, 42
Knoll International, 115, 118, 119
Kramer Brothers, 171
Kroll, Hammond, 111

Laminated woods, 68, 117, 124
Lancet arch, 54
Lannuier, Charles-Honoré, 43, 44
Leather: surface, 112; upholstery, 16, 17, 49, 100, 102, 104
Liebes, Dorothy, 113
Lion motif, 41, 82, 86, 138
Lotus motif, 89
Lozenge, 9
Lunette, 10

Machine banding, 56
McIntire, Samuel, 35
Maloof, Sam, 124
Marcotte, Leon, 73, 74, 76
Marquetry, 75, 94, 95
Marx, Samuel, 112
Mask (female head), 67, 79
Mathews, Lucia K. and Arthur F., 101
Medial stretcher, 17
Méridienne (daybed), 50
Mirror, 66, 123
Molding: astragal (bead), 8, (double), 22; cavetta, 22; channel, 11; cyma, 18; cyma reversa, 13; ogee, 99, 142; ovolo, 13, 150
Mortise-and-tenon joint, 140
Mullion, 38, 150
Muntin, 15, 141
Music cabinet, 85
Music rack, 121, 122

Nakashima, George, 164
Needlework upholstery, 58, 60
Nelson, Matter, and Company, 83
Niedecken Walbridge Company, 99
Noguchi, Isamu, 118
Nunns, Robert, 78

Oak-leaves-and-acorn motif, 68
Octagonal column, 56
Ogee arch, 53
Ogee molding, 99, 142
Orb, winged, 86
Ormolu, 43, 44, 49, 73, 74, 76, 82, 86
Ovolo molding, 13, 150

Pad foot, 24, 106, 142
Paintbrush foot, 11
Patera, 36
Paw foot, 25, 41, 44, 45
Pedestal, 81, 92
Pedestal support: card table, 48; chair, 119
Pediment: 18; broken arch (scrolled), 25, 29, 31, 133, 148, 150
Pembroke table, 37
Pendant, 14, 54
Perkins, Larry, 114
Phyfe, Duncan, style, 41, 50, 51
Piano, 78
Pier table, 51, 67
Pilaster, 38, 82, 134
Pimm, John, 25
Plastic, 119
Plinth, 55, 85
Poppy motif, 108
Portuguese foot, 11
Press cupboard, 9
Purcell, William, 96
Putti, 68

Quatrefoil, 53
Quervelle, Antoine Gabriel, 45

Rail (chair), front, side, 33
Rail (chest), 10
Reeding, 39, 46, 97
Reel turning, 14
Relief carving, 7, 108, 136, 141
Renwick, James, Jr., 54
Robert Wood and Company, 166
Rocking chair, 116, 153, 156, 162
Rococo carving, 29
Rohlfs, Charles, 105
Roman arch, 10
Rose, flowers and leaves, 64, 70
Rosette, 10, 139
Roux, Alexander, 67, 72, 75, 84
Rush seat, 144, 151, 158

S scroll, 63, 68, 169
Saarinen, Eero, 114, 115, 119
Saarinen, Eliel, 110
Savery, William, 146
Scallop shell, 25, 29, 63, 142, 148, 150, 151
Scroll foot, 48, 63, 65, 77, 81, 167, 170
Scrolled pediment (broken arch), 25, 29, 31, 133, 148, 150
Scott, Isaac E., 93
Scrutoir (desk), 21
Serpentine (curve), 34, 36, 63, 68
Settee, 41, 53, 161, 165, 169, 171
Shearer, John, 150
Shell. See Scallop
Shield-shaped back, 35
Shoe, 24, 33
Shonk (wardrobe), 131
Shoulder (chair), 24
Sideboard, 36
Skirt (apron), 11, 29, 67

Slat-back chair, 127, 144, 145, 156, 158
Slide, for candlestick, 20
Slipper foot, 27
Sofa, 71, 76, 77
Spade foot, 35
Spandrel (clock), 31, 148
Spanish foot, 11
Sphynx motif, 44, 86
Spindle, 1, 3, 5, 94, 140; split, 9, 59
Spiral turning, 13, 15, 58, 60, 62, 94
Splat, 27
Splay leg, 143
Splint seat, 3, 156
Split spindle, 9, 59
Stand, 107, 155
Stencil decoration, 151, 162
Stickley, Gustav, 104
Stile: chair, 17; chest, 10, 141
Stool, 8, 88, 89, 118
Strapwork, 7, 60, 78
Stretcher (side, front, medial), 17
Stringing, 37

Table, gate-leg, 18
Tassel motif, 79
Tea table, 26
Tester, 23
Tiffany Studios, 97
Tisch, Charles, 94
Tongue (slipper foot), 27
Trefoil, 52, 102
Trefoil arch, 52
Trestle base, 2, 129, 164
Triangle motif, 90, 136
Triphid foot, 146
Tulip motif, 135, 141
Tuscan column, 17

Urn, 35, 37, 47, 146, 168

Van Dorn Iron Works, 168
Veneer, 21
Volute, 27, 33, 159

W. P. A. Craft Project, Illinois, 114
Wardrobe, 126, 128, 131
Water leaf, 41
Wave pattern (classical), 32
Whiplash curve, 105
Wright, Ambrose, 52
Wright, Frank Lloyd, 100

Yoke (chair), 24, 146